3D Patterns for the Scroll Saw

by Diana Thompson

Acknowledgements

Thanks to my Lord for His guidance and the gift that gives me so much joy.

Thanks to my husband, Capt. Bob, for his always unfailing support and encouragement. He never complained as I gradually took over every tool he owned.

Thank you Patrick Spielman. You always took the time to answer a beginner's questions and wouldn't let me get away with anything but my best.

A special thanks to my editor, Ayleen Stellhorn. She gives the creativity free reign.

Publisher: Alan Giagnocavo
Editor: Ayleen Stellhorn
Desktop Specialist: Linda L. Eberly, Eberly Designs Inc.
Cover Photography: Robert Polett
Cover Design: Linda Forrest

ISBN 1-56523-158-9
Library of Congress Card Number 2001088891

To order your copy of this book,
please remit the cover price
plus $3.00 shipping to:
Fox Chapel Publishing Company
Book Orders
1970 Broad Street
East Petersburg, PA 17520

Or visit us on the web at
www.scrollsawer.com

Printed in China
10 9 8 7 6 5 4 3 2

Table of Contents

Introduction

This book came into being because of my love for the art of scroll sawing. From my very first try, I knew this was going to be a life-long joy. Similar to the game of golf, the scroll sawing has become a passion. Some things just grab us and hold on forever.

About a year ago, I discovered compound sawing on a web site and decided to give it a try. From that first tiny figure, I fell in love with the total concept. In my search for more patterns, I discovered there weren't a whole lot available. That led to my first attempts at designing my own patterns.

I have to admit, designing patterns was harder than I had imagined. One failed pattern attempt followed another until I began to learn what would work, what wouldn't, and what had possibilities if I worked with it long enough. I have a bucket full of pieces that were supposed to work, looked like they should work, but didn't—and I smile every time I look at them. For instance, there's a bunny near the top of the pile that came out with four ears. He looks like he's having a bad hair day. And there's a duck with one leg.... The mistakes are as much fun as the successes, and I do enjoy laughing at myself when something comes out goofy. It's all a learning process.

The inspirations for the designs come from everywhere. The mailbox idea came while sitting at my computer

Rob's Gooney, pattern on page 34.

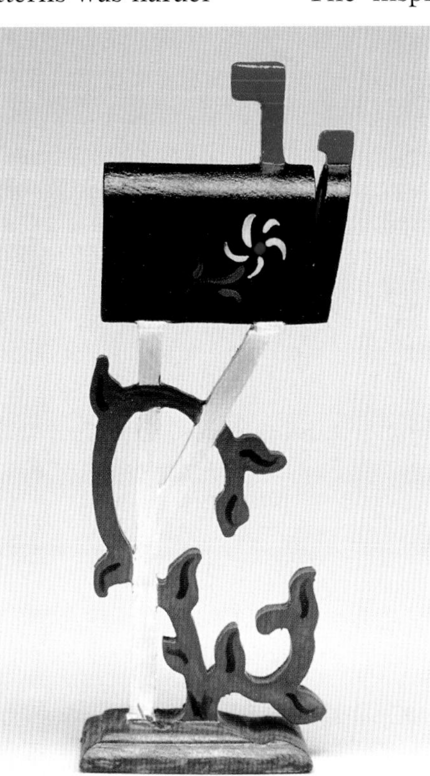

Mailbox, pattern on page 10.

Boo's Egret, pattern on page 17.

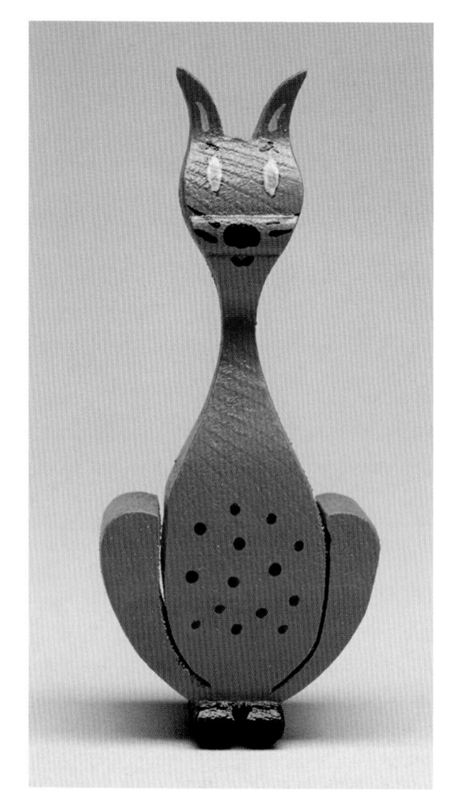

Mr. Whiskers, pattern on page 29.

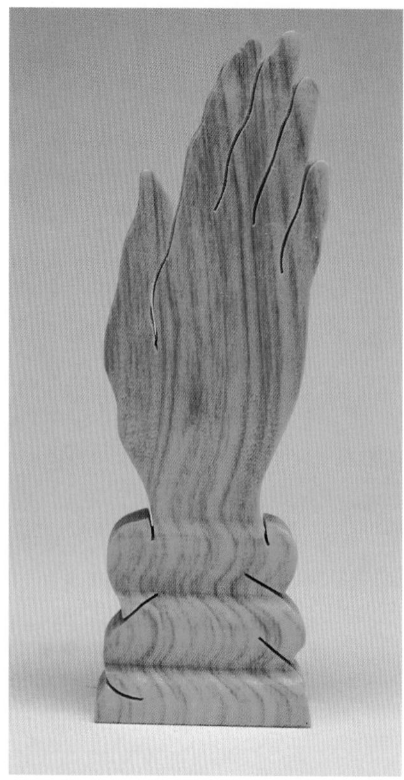

Thankful Hands, pattern on page 39.

Songbird, pattern on page 37.

in the mornings looking out the window at my own mailbox. The songbird came into being from listening to the birds sing every morning. *Boo's Egret* was born from a photograph my son took while out fishing. *Rob's Gooney* was an idea from a cheerful note my daughter sent me. *Mr. Whiskers* is my son-in-law Rick's beloved, silly cat.

Some ideas come when I least expect them. *Thankful Hands* was inspired while saying my prayers. I was having trouble drawing a hand and happened to look at my own hands as they were folded in prayer. I traced around them, and there was the pattern! All the bumps and imperfections were left in, just as they appear on my own imperfect hands.

I keep a notebook with me at all times, just in case a new idea presents itself. There have been a number of days when I came home from playing golf with ideas written down all over my score card. It's like I look at the world in a whole new way and everything has the possibility of being a design. When a new idea comes along I can hardly wait to get started on it. Seeing the little figures come out of the block just makes my heart happy.

One of the most wonderful results of my work is having my friends and family become involved. They are always on the alert for new ideas. And it's so marvelous to see the smiles on their faces when they see a figure made from one of their ideas.

I beg forgiveness from all of you who know how to paint, of which I am not one. I've been told I should not be allowed to own a paint brush. I have a tendency to be whimsical in my choice of colors, hence the lavender *Mr. Whiskers* and the orange cat. These are my humble efforts to embellish the figures—and it's all part of the 3-D fun. You never know what will come out of your own imagination.

It is my hope that those of you who honor me by using my designs will enjoy making them as much as I enjoy bringing them to life.

—Diana Thompson

(scrollergirl@aol.com)

Getting Started

Rob's Gooney, pattern on page 34.

The figures in this book are made with a simple technique that turns out spectacular effects. Sometimes called 3-D scrolling, compound scrolling or sculpture scrolling, the cutting technique used in this method of scroll sawing gives your finished project three dimensions: height, width and depth. The result is a free-standing figure ready to delight and amuse.

Patterns

Right off the bat, anyone new to compound scrolling will notice that the patterns are very different from those used in traditional scrolling and fretwork. Each compound pattern has two parts: a front view and a profile view. These two views are separated by a dividing line. To use the pattern, simply fold it along the dividing line and wrap it around two sides of the wood. Two cuts are made on each figure: the front view and then the profile view. It's a simple technique that turns out some spectacular effects.

Choosing Your Tools

Scroll saws range in price anywhere from a couple hundred dollars to more than a thousand dollars. Make sure you try out a number of scroll saws and talk to other scrollers about their experiences before you buy a saw. My top three requirements for a scroll saw are durability, variable speed control and a quick blade-changing mechanism. Any brand of scroll saw will be able to handle the compound cuts required for the figures in this book.

A rotary tool, installed in a drill press attachment, is quite handy for drilling starter holes. It will ensure the starter holes are perfectly vertical. However, a hand drill can be used just as well.

A belt sander, if available, is excellent for beveling the angles of the barn pieces in the *Barnyard Project* on page 48 and the base of *Mr. and Mrs. Santa Music Box* on page 53.

Wood Choice

In the past, I cut all of the figures I planned to paint from white pine, but I have since discovered sugar pine. This is the easiest wood I've used for compound sawing—and my favorite.

If you are new to compound scrolling, I suggest starting out with sugar pine, white pine or basswood. All three are all fairly soft and easy to cut. In addition, white pine is readily available at most home improvement stores. Try to pick out a "clear" piece with a small grain and no knots.

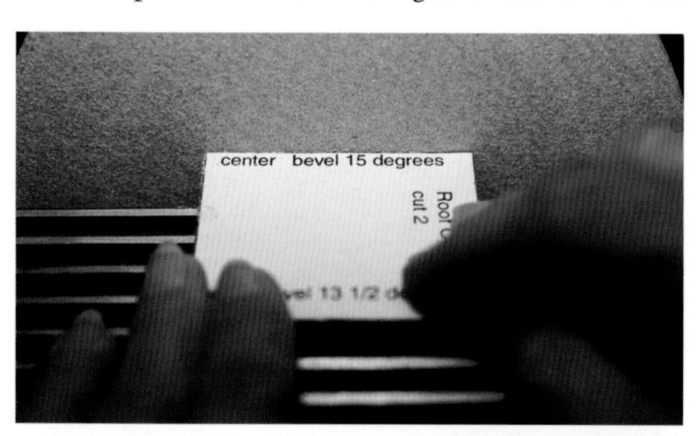

A belt sander can be used to ensure the bottom of the piece is square.

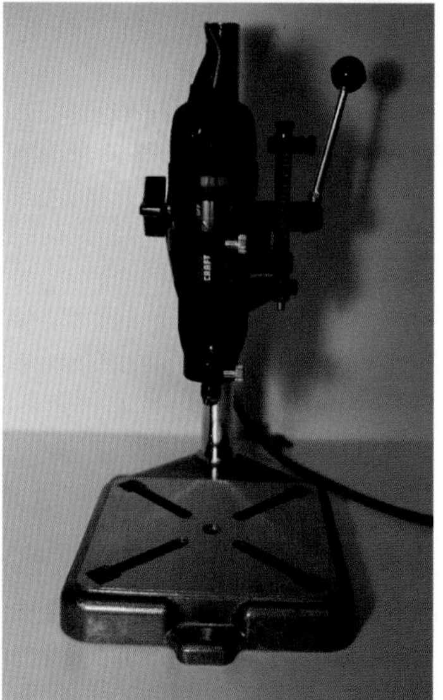
Use a drill press with a rotary tool to make perfectly vertical starter holes.

Knots will often tear out while you are cutting, ruining the figures.

The list below describes some of my favorite woods. Don't limit yourself, however, to the woods listed here. Try whatever strikes your fancy. Some will work well, others won't—but it's fun and educational to experiment.

A tip here about cutting the harder woods. Cover the stock with clear packing tape before applying the pattern. The adhesive in the tape helps to lubricate the blade and eliminates the potential for scorching the wood. I apply the tape directly to the wood, then apply the pattern. Applying tape on top of the pattern will cause a glare under work lights, making it difficult to see the blade as you cut.

Caution: Keep in mind that any wood dust can be an irritant to the respiratory system. Some woods, especially red cedar, redwood and most exotics, are toxic. Wear a dust mask when cutting and use a dust collection system. (The asterisks note woods that I have found especially troublesome.)

Soft woods

Sugar Pine: Very easy to work with. Finishes nicely. Very light in color.

Basswood: Very easy to cut, but takes a little more effort to get a smooth finish. Very light in color.

White Pine: Easy to cut and finish. Light in color.

Spanish Cedar: Easy to cut. Reddish brown in color with interesting flecks of color. Has a very distinctive aroma.

Medium woods

Willow: A little more difficult to cut, but one of my favorites. Tan to pinkish color, and often has a very pretty grain.*

Redwood: Usually dark in color. Easy to finish.*

Red Cedar: Beautiful red color, pleasant to work with and smells great!*

A wide variety of woods can be used with spectacular results. Left to right: sugar pine, Lauan, cyprus, Spanish cedar, poplar and red cedar.

Rob's Gooney, cut from old fence board.

Alder: Another of my favorites. Caramel in color. Very easy to finish.
Cyprus: Interesting light to dark grains. Reminds me of a zebra.
Poplar: Nice to work with and finishes nicely. Color varies from white to green to tan, depending from which part of the tree the wood is taken.

Hard woods

Black Walnut: A deep dark color ranging from chocolate to almost ebony. One of my very favorites. Difficult to cut, but made easier with packing tape! Finishes beautifully.
Magnolia: From white to gray with interesting grains. Very dense but another of my favorites. Finishes beautifully.
Mahogany: A deep rich reddish-brown color. Finishes beautifully.*
Lauan: A type of mahogany, but lighter in color. Finishes nicely.
Red Oak: Lovely light red color. Finishes nicely.*
Marupa: Almost white with darker gray flecks. It doesn't finish well and usually turns yellow regardless of finish used.

Found wood can also be used for three-dimensional figures. *Rob's Gooney* (above) was cut from a pressure-treated fence board. **Caution:** Wood dust from pressure-treated wood contains chemicals that may be hazardous to your health if inhaled. Wear a dust mask when cutting this wood.

Tools

- Scroll saw
- #5 single or skip tooth blades
- Rotary tool with drill press attachment or hand drill
- 1/16" drill bit
- 1/4" drill bit
- 3/4" Scotch Tape
- Small screw driver
- Stationary belt sander (optional)
- 2 small clamps (optional)
- Hook tooth blades (optional)

Cutting aids

- Plexiglass
- Spray adhesive
- 3/4" two-sided tape or masking tape
- Carpenters glue
- Blade lubricant (optional)
- Odd blocks of stock (optional)
- Scraps of cardboard (optional)
- Proportional scale (optional)
- Packing tape (optional)

Finishing supplies

- Various grits of sandpaper (220 and 150 are the most frequently used grits)
- Wood sealer
- Acrylic craft paints
- Clear spray finish
- Danish oil

A ruler will help to check the blade's alignment.

Helpful Hints

• *Check your saw before you begin.* Check the tilt of your saw table, making sure it is set on zero tilt. If the saw table is off zero by the slightest amount, the figure will be skewed to one side or the other. The tilt of the table may also cause some parts to be eliminated from the final piece.

Also check the blade alignment to make sure the blade is perfectly straight. A misaligned blade will also result in an imperfectly cut figure. To check blade alignment, lay a thin ruler up against the left side of the blade and gently move the blade up and down by hand. If the ruler moves to the left during the stroke, the blade needs to be adjusted. Refer to your owner's manual for brand-specific instructions for making the adjustment. Each brand of saw will be different.

• *Use clamps as you cut.* I've found that clamping spare pieces of stock to each side of the work will hold the piece straight and help to prevent imperfectly cut figures—especially when cutting the thicker side of the pattern. The clamps give the work in progress more stability and give me a little more wood to hold, which makes for better maneuverability as well as safe fingers. Tighten the clamps only enough to hold your work in place and not so tight that they interfere with the blade moving through the kerf.

To check that the clamps aren't too tight, try backing your moving blade into a kerf. If it won't go easily, then the clamps are too tight After a little practice, you will soon learn exactly when the clamps are just right. Also make sure your piece doesn't "wobble" once the clamps are applied. If it does, reposition the clamps until your work is lying flat against the table.

Working with clamps may seem a little awkward at first, but you will soon get used to it and may even find, like I did, that you prefer cutting this way.

• *Choose your blades appropriately.* I recommend cutting all the figures in this book with a #5 plain, single tooth or skip tooth blade. A larger blade doesn't have the maneuverability needed and a smaller blade will break too easily when cutting

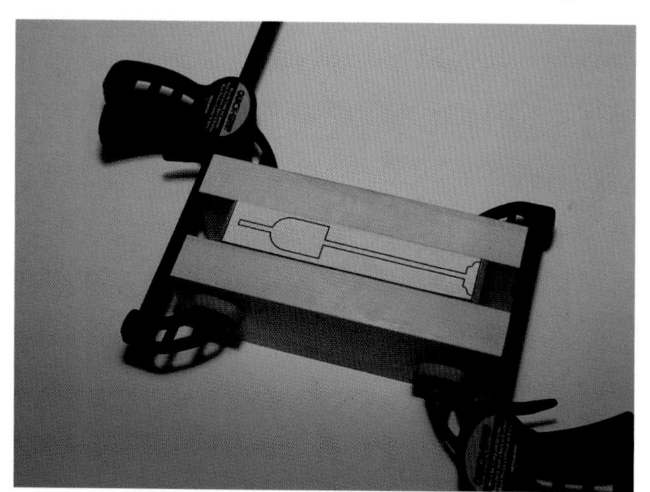

Extra holding room is created with blocks and clamps.

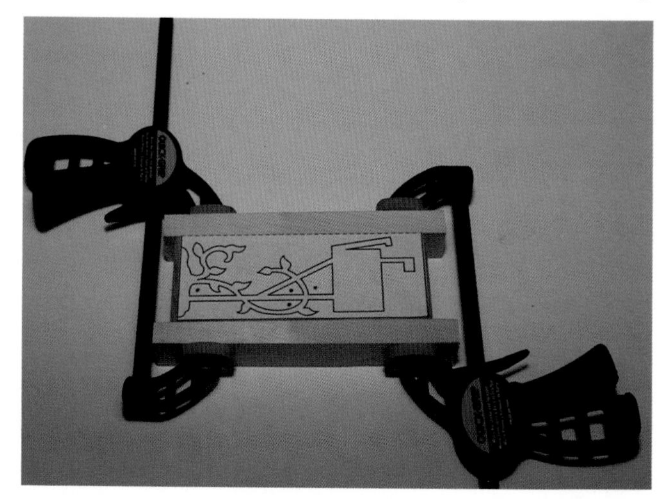

Clamps also provide stability during cuts on the second side.

the thicker sides of the patterns. There are many brands of blades available. Some are more aggressive and faster than others. Experiment and choose a blade that fits your skill level. I recommend avoiding reverse tooth blades, as they have a tendency to slow down the cutting action when cutting thicker wood.

Change your blade often. Most blades will cut two figures, if not more, depending on the type wood you use. The softer the wood, the longer the blade will last. If your blade breaks in the middle that usually means it has become dull. I've found that using a blade lubricant makes the work go smoother and helps the blades to last a little longer. The wax also keeps the blade cleaner. Push the stick into the running blade until the teeth are well coated.

I use a hook-tooth blade for cutting my stock to size. This blade is designed for cutting thicker stock. It lasts forever, cuts very fast, and saves wear and tear on the #5 blades. Hook-tooth blades come in two sizes: I use the smaller one, which has seven teeth per inch.

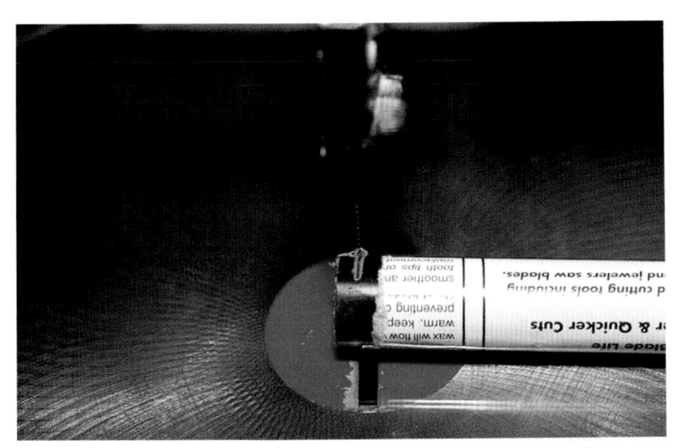

Blade lubricant is an optional accessory that may help to lengthen the life of your blades.

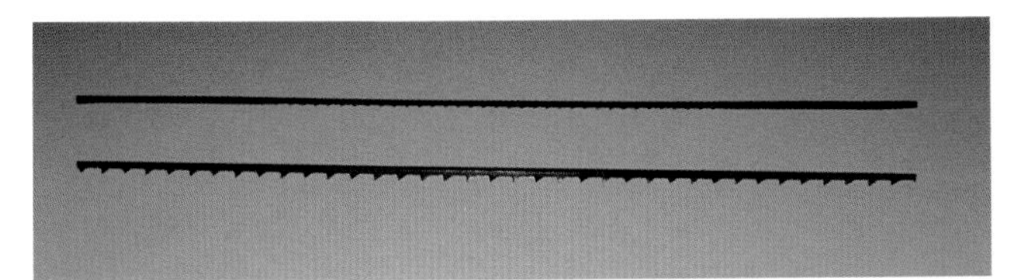

No. 5 single or skip tooth blades are ideal for compound cutting.

• *Cut carefully.* For the best results, saw to the waste side of the lines. Some of the pattern lines are very narrow and delicate, such as the wings on the lacy butterfly pattern and the vine on the mailbox pattern. If you saw directly on the lines, too much wood is removed and breaking may occur.

When turning sharp corners and curves, don't be afraid to be aggressive. The saw blade is not as delicate as you might think. It will take a lot of pulling in all directions. I've found that it will do most anything I ask of it. The one thing you don't want to do is push the blade sideways. This will result in a lopsided figure.

• *Buy carefully.* Take a small ruler with you when buying stock. I've often come home with what I thought was ¾-inch wood and found that it wasn't. Thicker will work fine, but thinner won't. All but one pattern, Attitude Cat, page 15, calls for ¾-inch-thick stock. When thicker stock is required, as with the tulip, pear and apple patterns, two pieces of wood, ¾-inch-thick, can be glued together with carpenters glue and clamped in place until set.

• *Use the trapping method.* For cutting the smaller figures, such as the candle for the lamppost or the Christmas presents, it is important to keep all the small pieces together. Once a piece slips out, it can slide through the blade hole, or fly out onto the floor and be gone forever in the accumulated debris that finds its way to the shop floor.

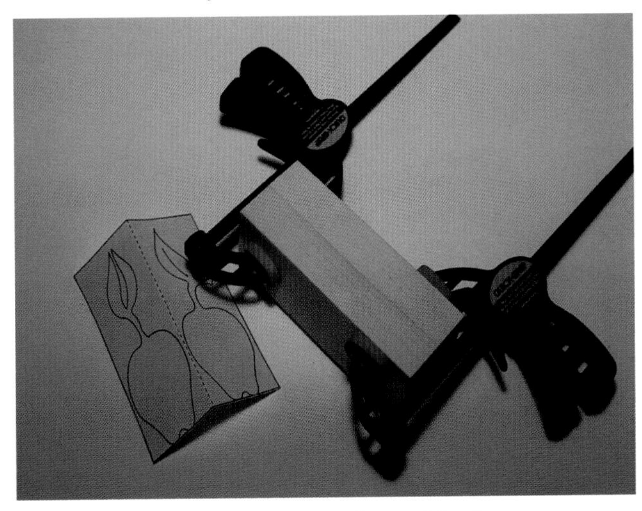

Glue up and clamp two pieces of wood for larger patterns.

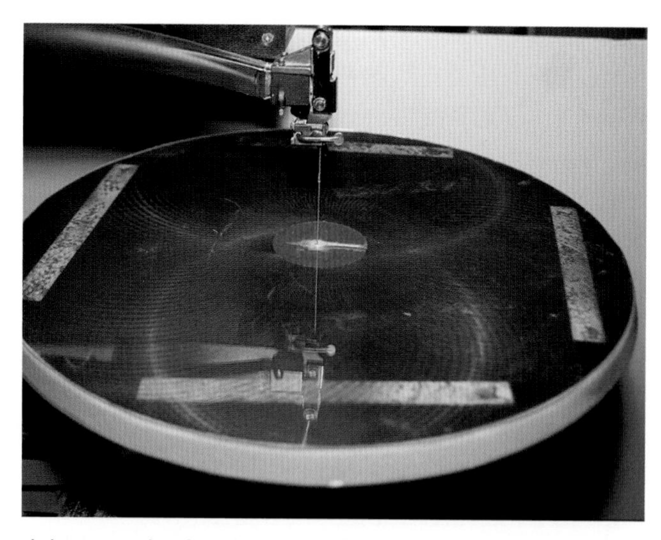

A homemade plexiglass saw table covering makes the surface super smooth.

I use what I call the trapping method. This method traps the tiny pieces inside the blocks and keeps them from slipping out while cutting. Simply use a good brand of tape or clamps to keep the pieces in place while you make the second cut.

• *Choose a good spray glue.* There are several brands on the market and your choice is simply a matter of preference. Because the pattern is not removed from the stock, it doesn't matter how much spray adhesive you use. It's better to have too much glue. Using too little glue will cause the pattern to work loose as you're cutting.

• *Use reference materials.* The best tip I could

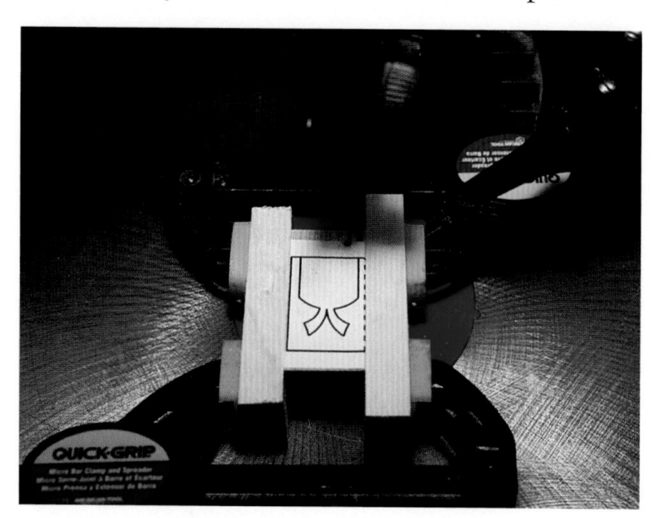

Cut in from the edge or drill a starter hole to begin cutting your piece.

give anyone, especially beginning scrollers, is to purchase a good book on basic scroll sawing techniques. Look for a book that covers all areas of scroll sawing, gives lots of helpful advice and provides practice exercises that can be done on any scroll saw to help you hone your skills.

Finishing Techniques

There are several ways to finish the figures. I must admit that my strong point is not painting. It's an art that seems to elude me, however hard I try. I've painted the figures to give some idea of how they can be embellished. Feel free to experiment with your own ideas.

If you're planning to paint the figures, I would suggest using sugar pine or white pine for cutting stock. You wouldn't want to cover up a beautiful hardwood with paint. Gently sand each figure with 220-grit paper. Coat them with your choice of wood sealer, and allow them to dry thoroughly. Sealer not only makes a good painting surface, it also adds some extra strength to the more delicate patterns.

If I plan to use a spray finish on the hardwoods, I also use a sealer beforehand for them also. After sealing, sand smooth, again using 220-grit paper. Rolled and folded sandpaper of different thicknesses makes for an easier job.

After each figure is painted, I use a clear spray to give each a finished look. Yellowing of the colors is a real concern, especially if you are using white paint. Test the finish on a scrap piece of painted wood before you use it on your compound piece. A handy tip for ease of clear coating: Spray a piece of cardboard with spray adhesive, stick the figure to it, then spray the figure with the clear finish. The cardboard gives you the extra grip you need and allows the figure to be turned as needed for full coverage—without getting fingerprints all over it.

The hardwoods are most beautiful when left natural. I use Danish oil to finish the natural pieces. It brings out the beauty of the wood and is a very simple finishing method. Follow the directions on the product you choose to use.

Techniques

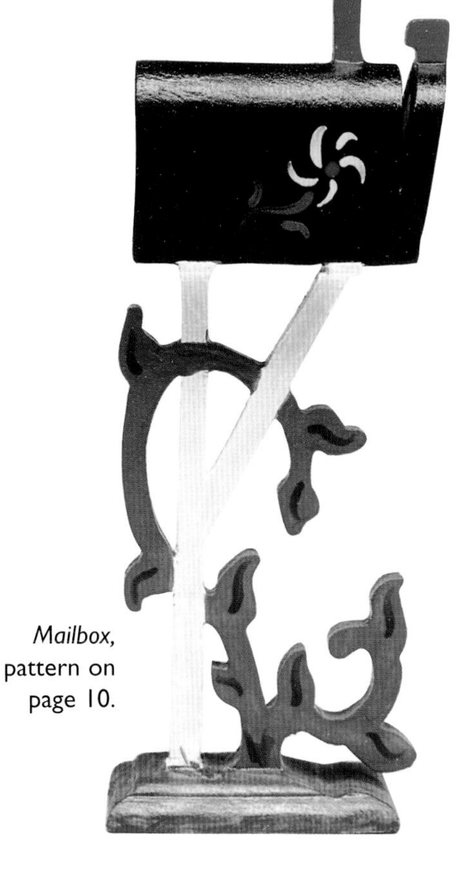

Mailbox, pattern on page 10.

This is where it all comes together. In the step-by-step demonstration that follows, you will find all the steps needed to cut a prefect figure. I will show you a fail-safe way to line up the pattern and give you some trouble shooting tips that guarantee perfectly cut compound pieces every time. By the time your first figure falls out of the block, you will have discovered—just like I did—how easy 3-D sawing is and how much enjoyment it can bring.

Before You Begin

First, make photocopies or computer scans of the patterns. Beware that some copy machines are not always accurate, so measure the first copy to make sure it's the exact size of the original pattern. This is easily done with a ruler. Having an exact pattern is extremely important in compound sawing. Otherwise, the front and profile cuts may not match up correctly, resulting in a skewed piece.

Next, put a #5 blade in your saw, and do a check to make sure the saw is running properly, according to the owner's manual. Be sure to read through the safety tips provided by the manufacturer. Being comfortable with the operation of your scroll saw will make scrolling more enjoyable and help prevent many mishaps.

Finally, get out your safety gear. Always wear safety glasses when working with any machinery—scroll saws included. Dust and chips can fly and do serious damage to the eyes. I recommend a dust mask as well. Nearly every type of wood has a toxicity of some nature. Not everyone is sensitive to the toxins, but that doesn't mean you can't become so over time and length of exposure.

MAILBOX

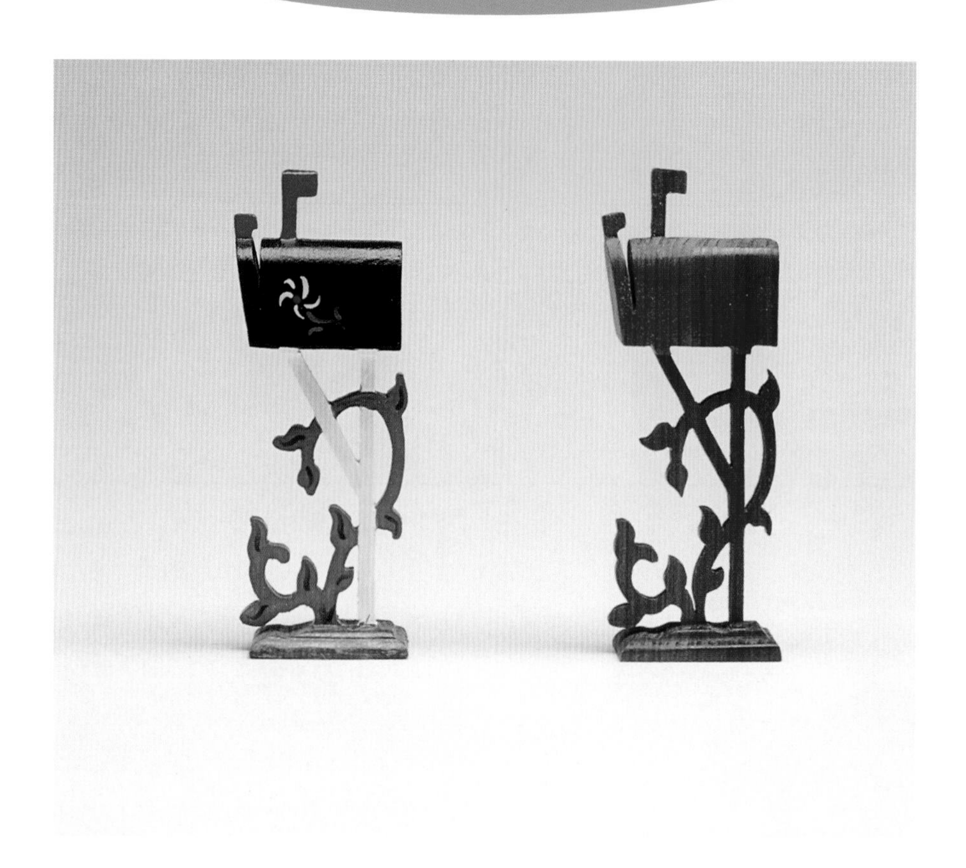

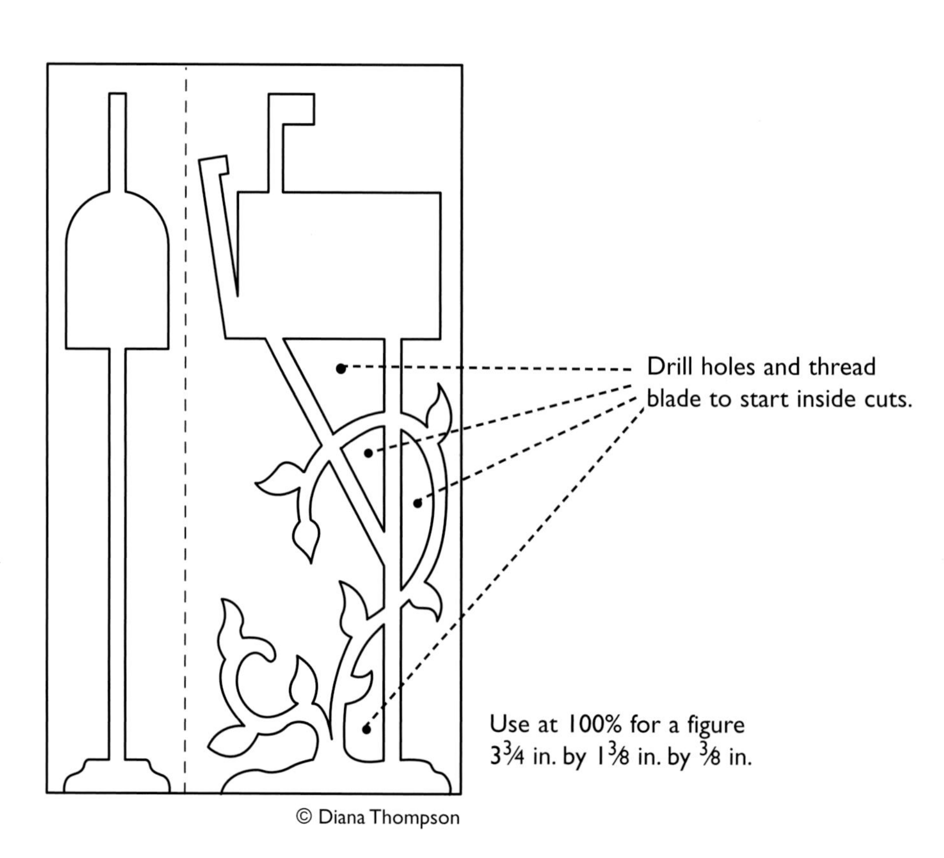
Drill holes and thread blade to start inside cuts.
Use at 100% for a figure $3\frac{3}{4}$ in. by $1\frac{3}{8}$ in. by $\frac{3}{8}$ in.

1 Trim the pattern to size. Do not cut along the dashed line between the front and side views.

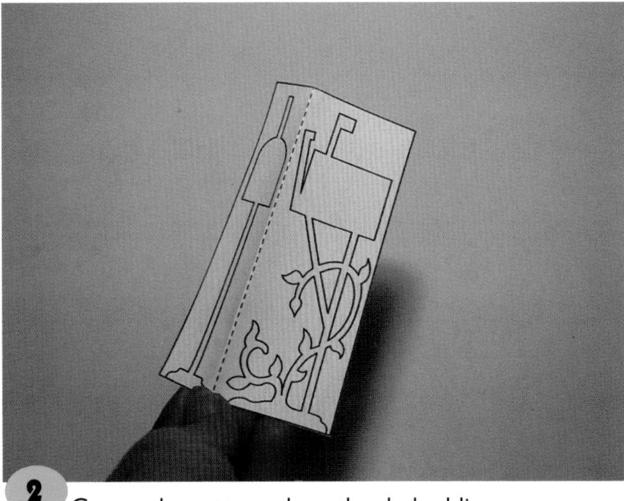

2 Crease the pattern along the dashed line.

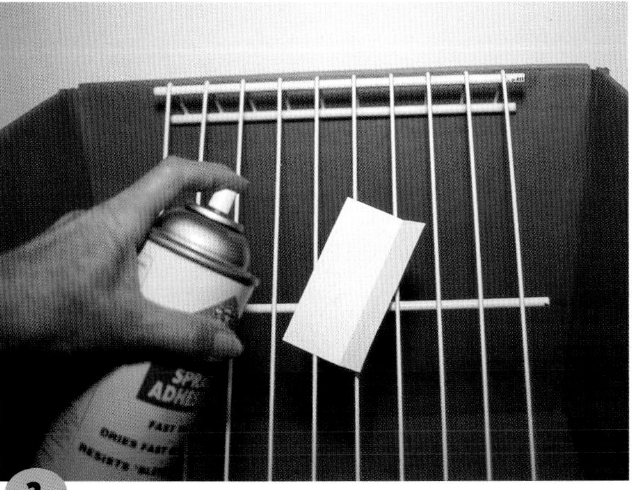

3 Spray the back of the pattern with adhesive. A cardboard box with a grate positioned inside at a 45 degree angle makes a great spray booth.

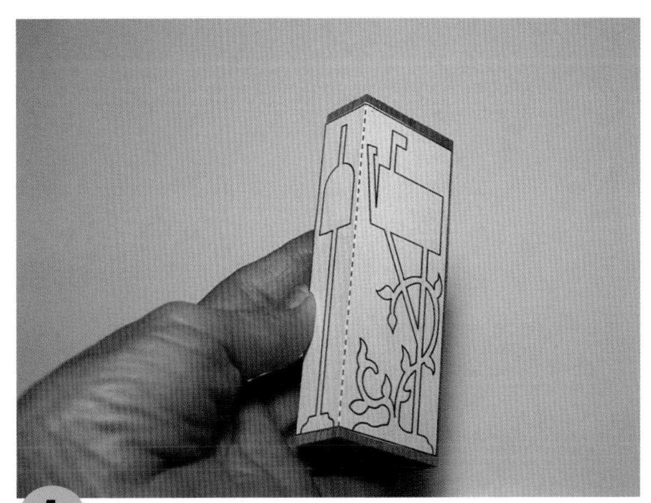

4 Use 3/4 in. stock. Wrap the pattern around two sides of the stock. Make sure that the dashed line runs straight along the edge of your stock.

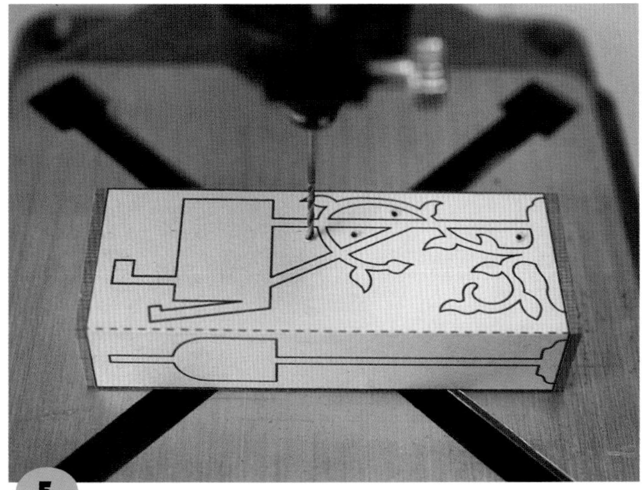

5 Drill starter holes as indicated. Tip: Placing a piece of scrap wood under your project while drilling starter holes will eliminate a lot of tear-out.

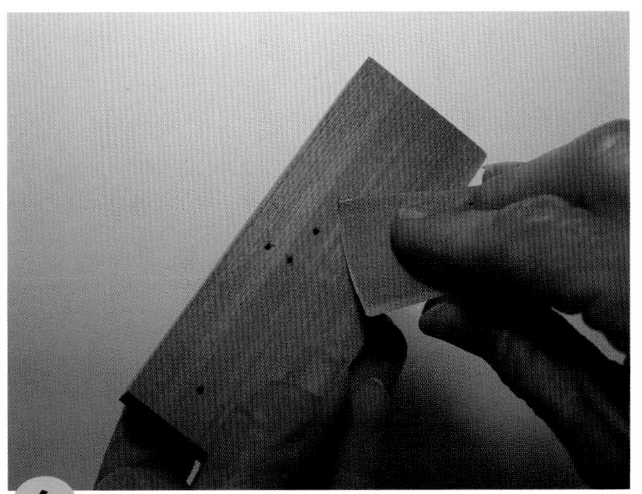

6 Sand away tear-outs on the reverse side of the stock.

Trouble Shooting

The most-often-asked question I hear about compound sawing is: "Why is my figure not the same on the bottom as it is on the top, even thought I followed the lines?"

First check out the mechanical reasons:

- Is the table saw sitting at an angle? If so, reset it at zero.
- Is your blade alignment straight? If not, realign the blade so it makes a straight cut.
- Are the pieces taped together too loosely, causing them to wobble? If yes, retape the block.
- Is the tension on the blade tight enough? You will find yourself pushing extremely hard while cutting if the tension is off.

All that being said, the major cause of lopsided figures is operator induced: pushing the blade sideways as you cut. Many beginning scrollers do not even realize they are pushing against the blade. To avoid this pitfall, make sure you are feeding the wood straight into the blade. Another indicator of pushing the blade sideways is that the saw bulks at making the rather sharp turns. When you feel this happening, ease up and let the blade right itself, then continue cutting. After a little while, you will become aware of what is happening, and you will automatically ease up on the blade.

Caution

Every scroll saw comes equipped with a foot to hold the wood in place. Check the manufacturer's recommendations and cautions if you decide to remove the hold-down foot. If you choose to remove the hold-down foot, be sure to keep your hands well away from the moving blade and hold the wood down firmly against the table top. A loose hold will cause the wood to jump and may do damage to the artwork, your hands, the saw or all of the above.

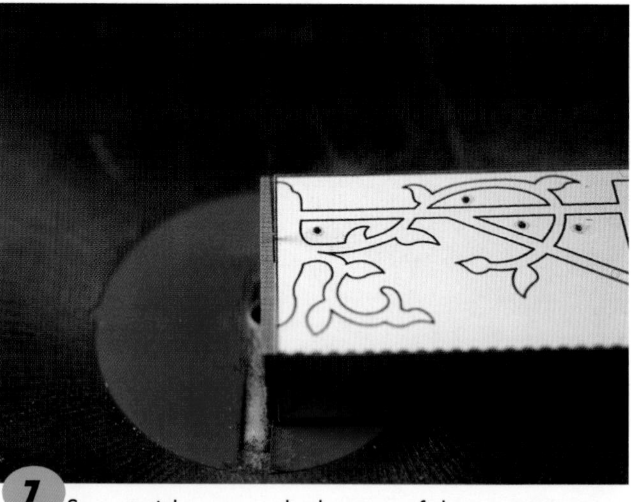

7 Saw straight across the bottom of the pattern . . .

8 . . . or sand the bottom square with a belt sander.

9 Make all the inside cuts first, remembering to cut to the waste side of the lines. Leave the frets inside the block to give it extra stability and to keep the first cut from shifting when you make the second cut.

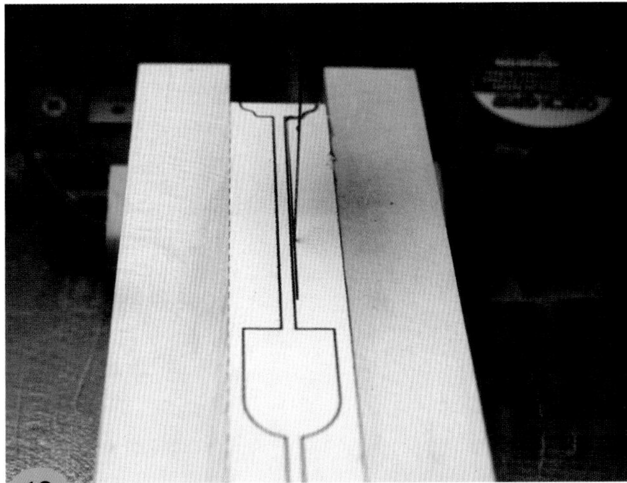

10 Cut the left side of the pattern first. (If you're using a pattern with a space between the legs, make that cut first. Then continue cutting the left side in one continuous line.)

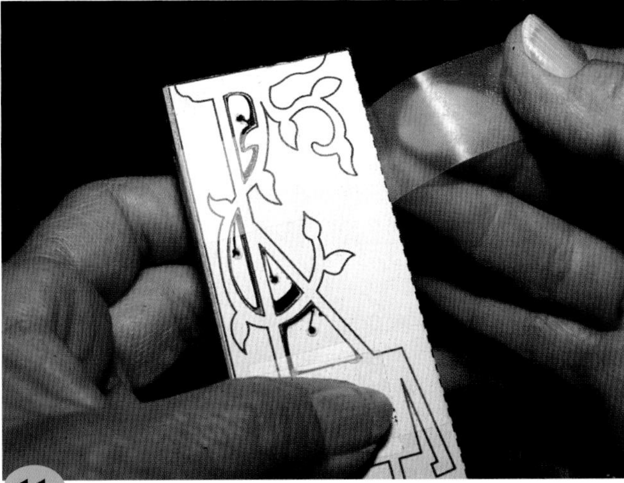

11 Replace any frets that fell out. Allowing the figure to rest naturally in the block, gently pinch the entire block together and tape the wood in place across the top and bottom with clear tape.

12 Cut the right side of the pattern in one, continuous line. As you cut this side, some of your frets may begin to fall out. This is not a problem at this stage of the process.

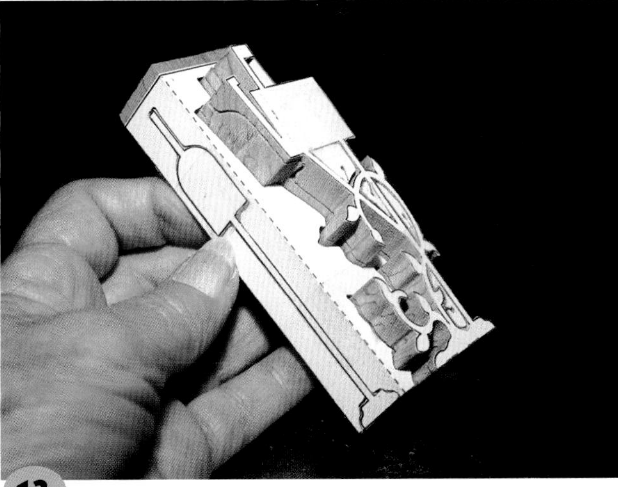

13 Gently push from behind to remove the figure from the block.

14 Remove the waste wood.

15 Like a box of Cracker Jacks™, there's a surprise inside.

Painting Technique

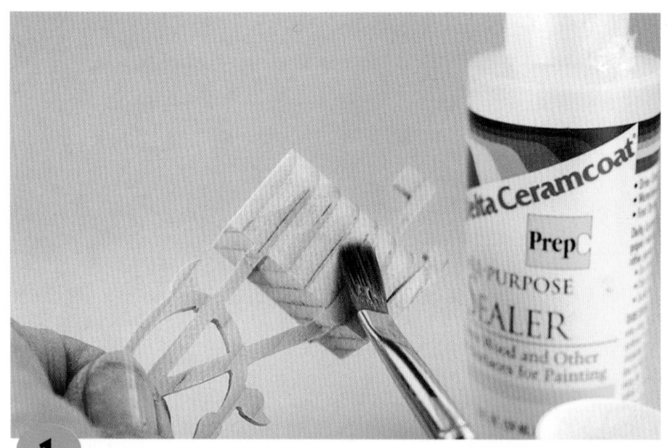

1 Apply a sealer to the figure. The sealer creates a smooth surface for painting and adds strength to the more fragile parts of the figure.

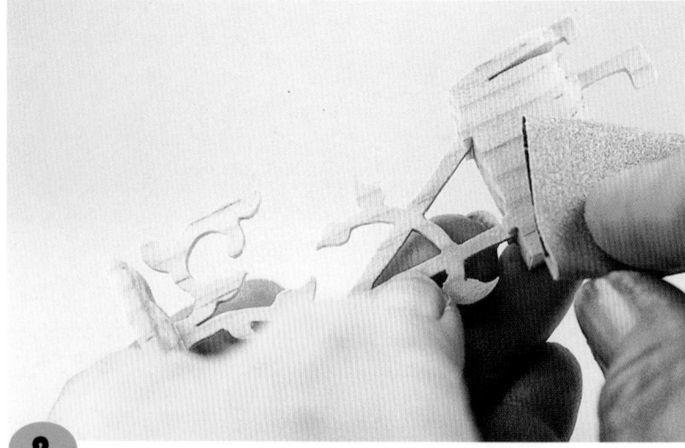

2 When the sealer is completely dry, sand the figure smooth with 220-grit sandpaper.

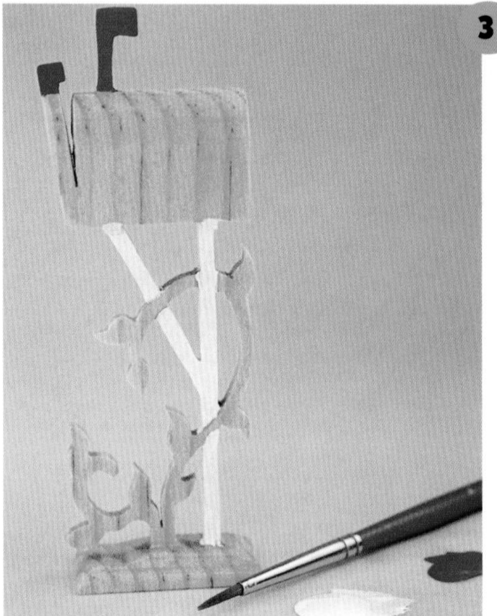

3 Apply the white and red paints. Both can be done at the same time because they don't touch each other. Two coats are usually enough. Allow the paint to dry as noted on the manufacturer's label.

4 Apply the green and black paints.

5 Thin the brown paint with a little water and paint the base. One coat is enough. If the black paint is dry, decorate the mailbox with your own name and address or another design of you choice.

6 Once your figure is dry, mount it on a piece of cardboard with spray adhesive. Apply two coats of clear spray finish.

ATTITUDE CAT

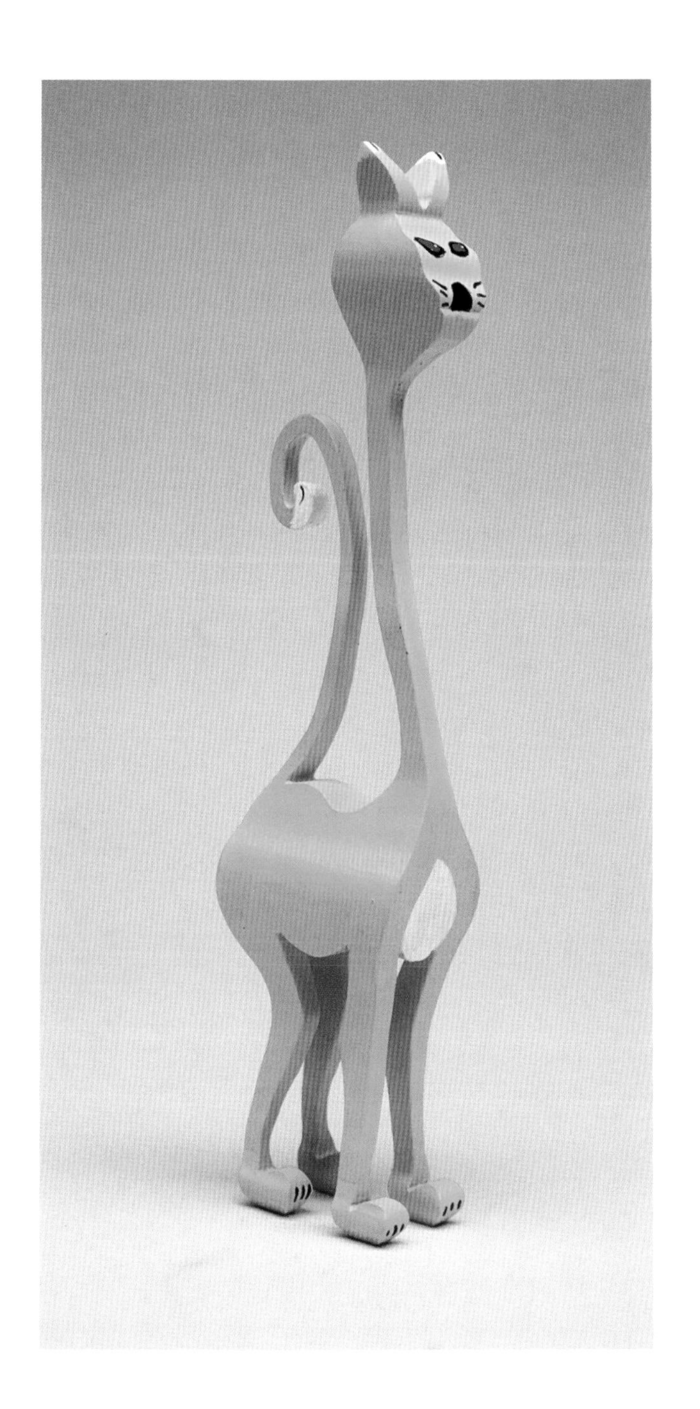

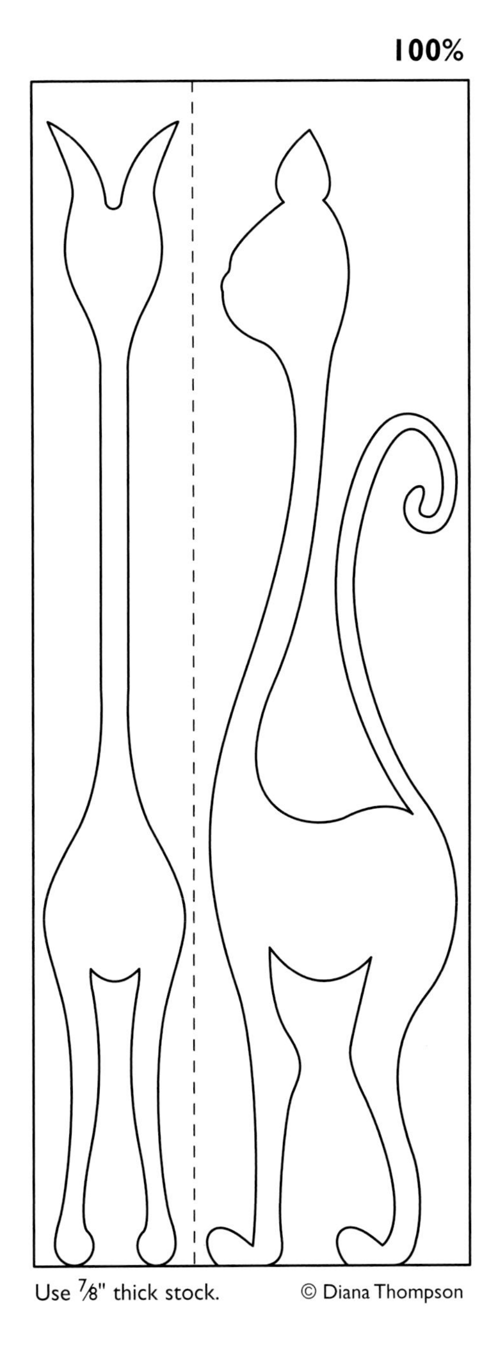

Use 7⁄8" thick stock.

BOOKWORM

100%

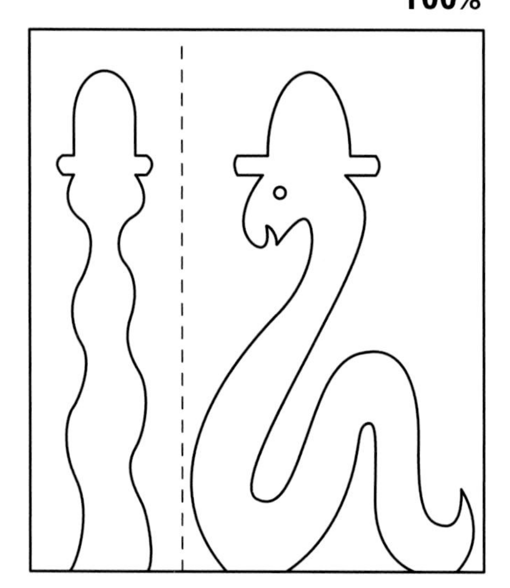

100%

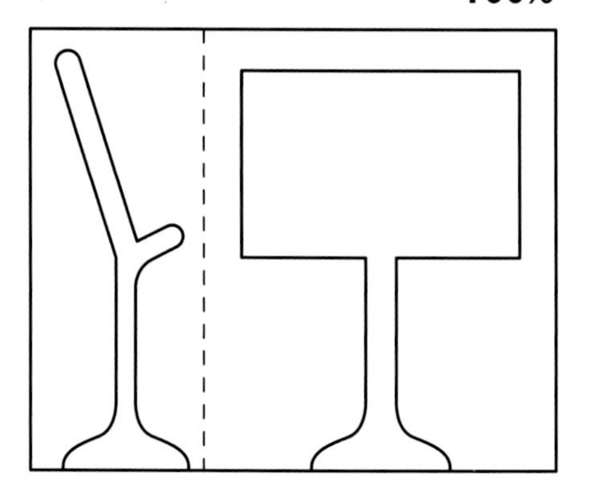

100%

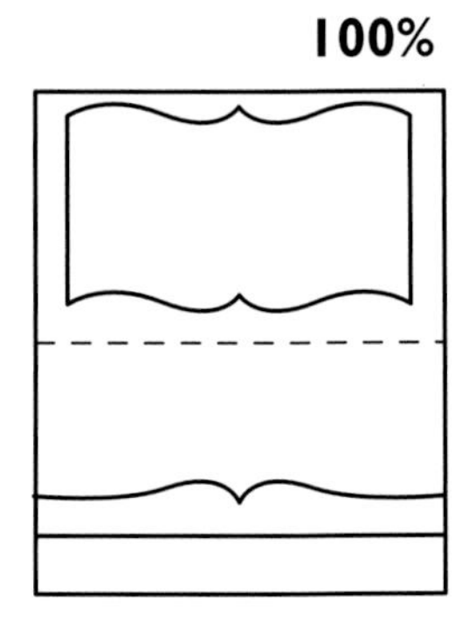

BOO'S EGRET

100%

© Diana Thompson

BUTTERFLY

100%

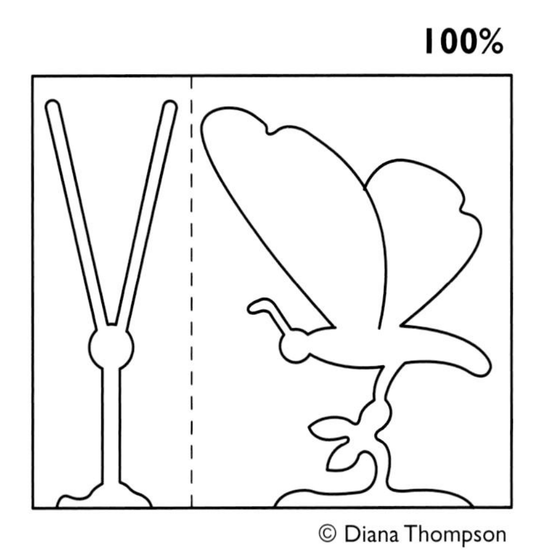

© Diana Thompson

CACTUS

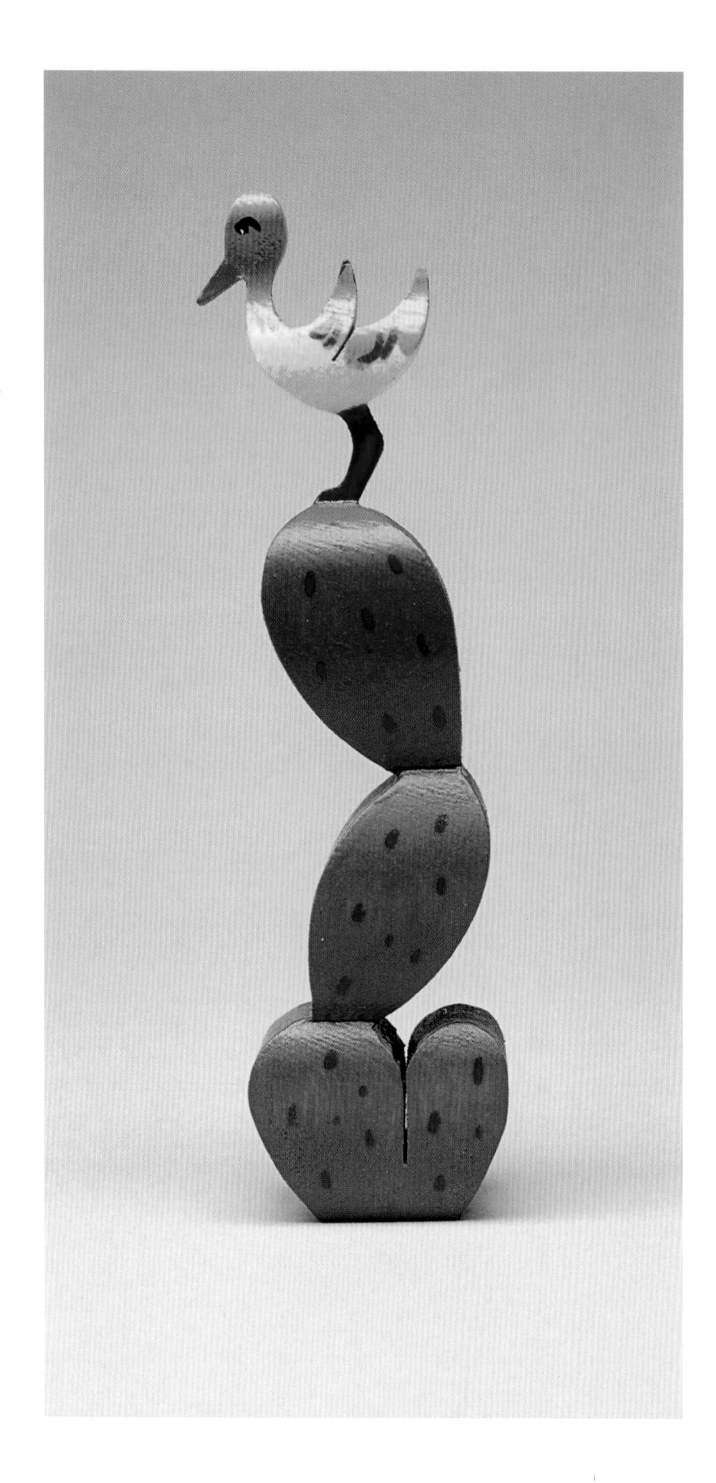

100%

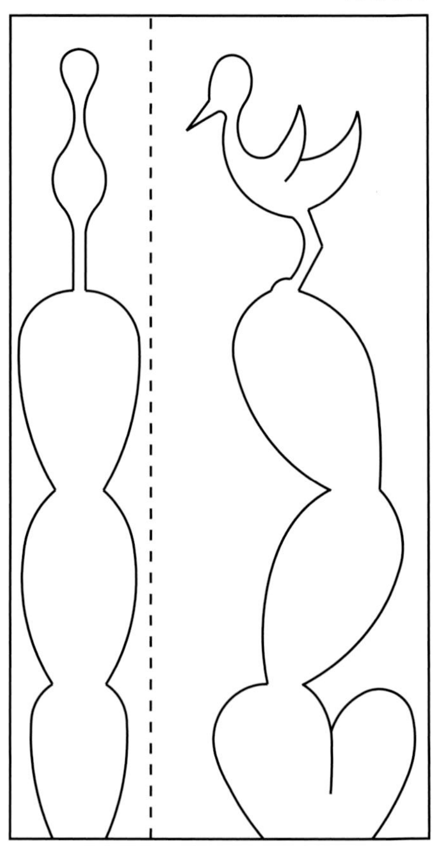

CHRISTMAS CANDLE

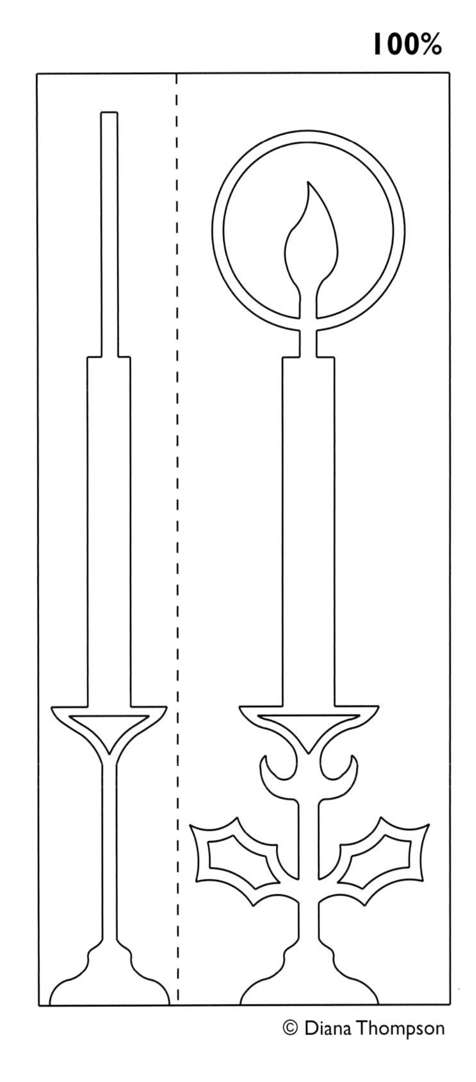

CHRISTMAS TREE

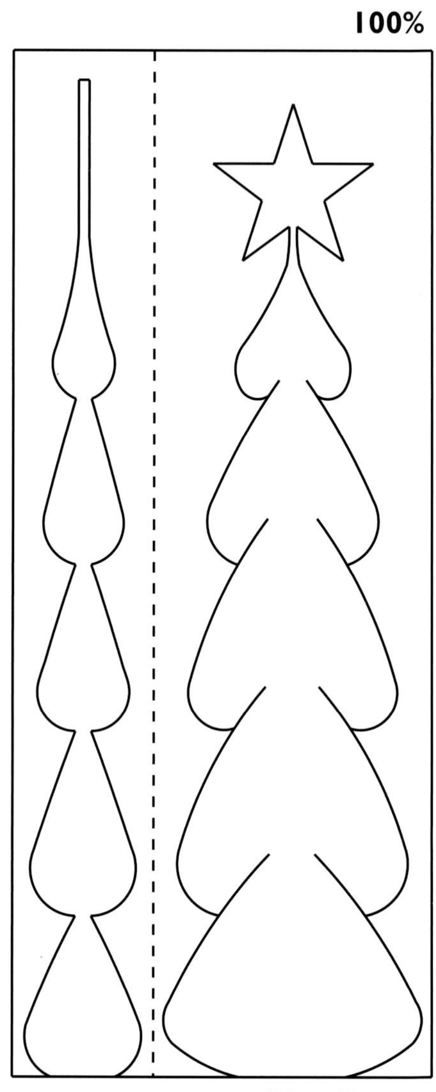

EASTER BASKET

EASTER BUNNY

FRUIT - APPLE

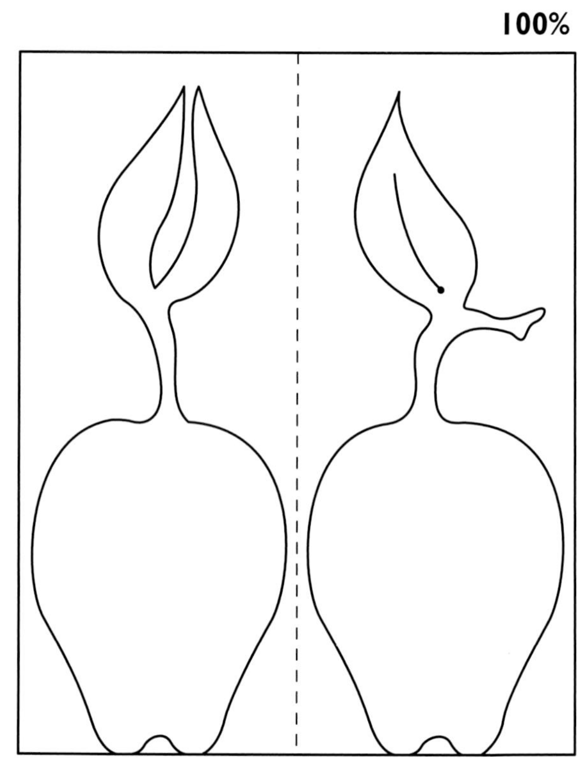

FRUIT - CHERRIES

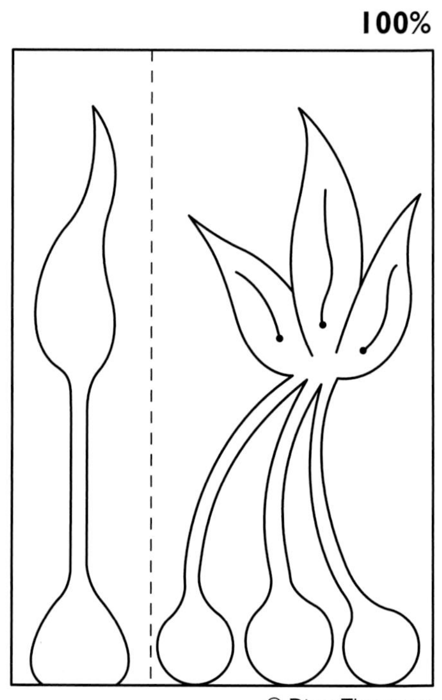

FRUIT - PEAR

100%

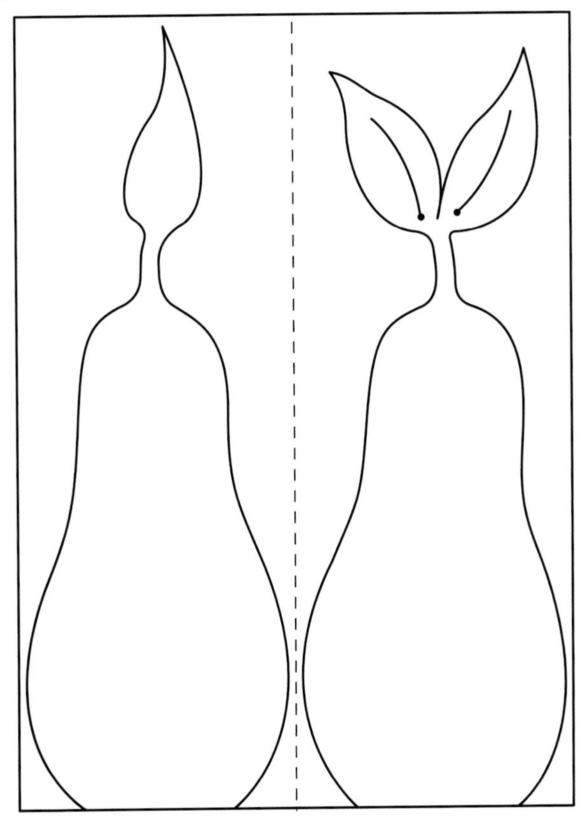

GHOST

100%

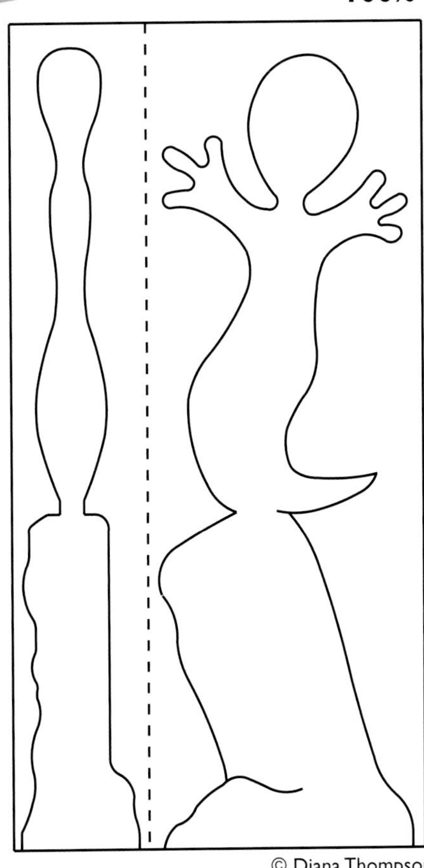

GOLF BAG

100%

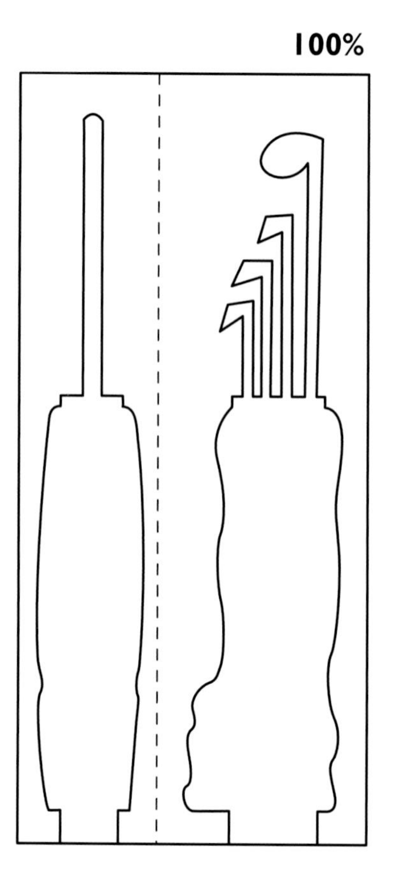

(extra club) 100%

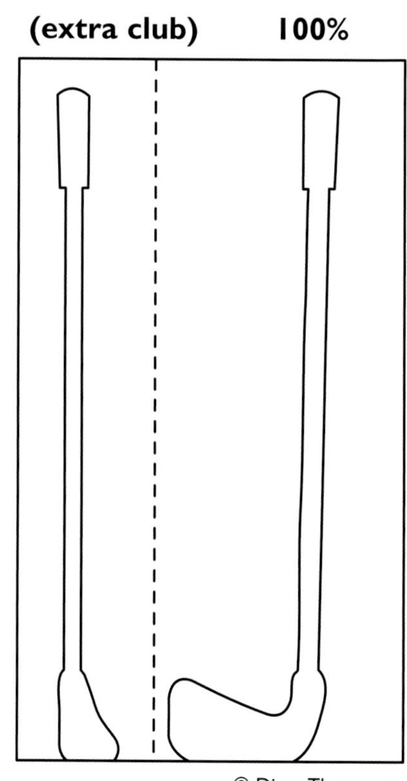

HEARTS

100%

KEY TO MY HEART

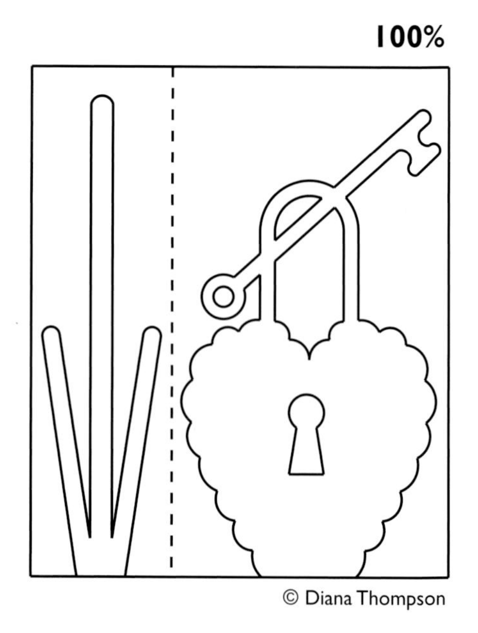

LACE BUTTERFLY

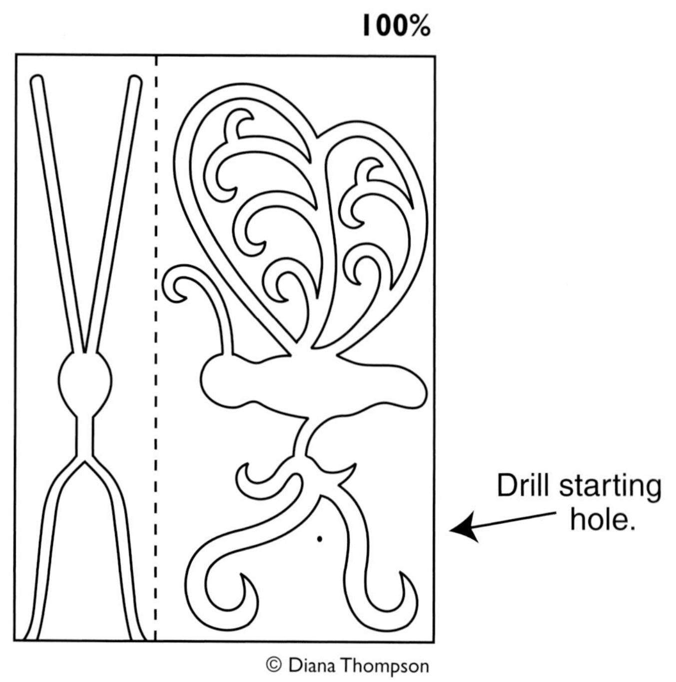

LADDER

100%

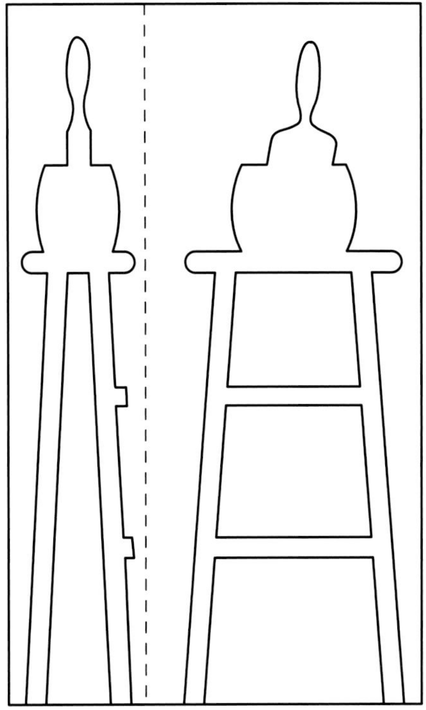

LAMPPOST

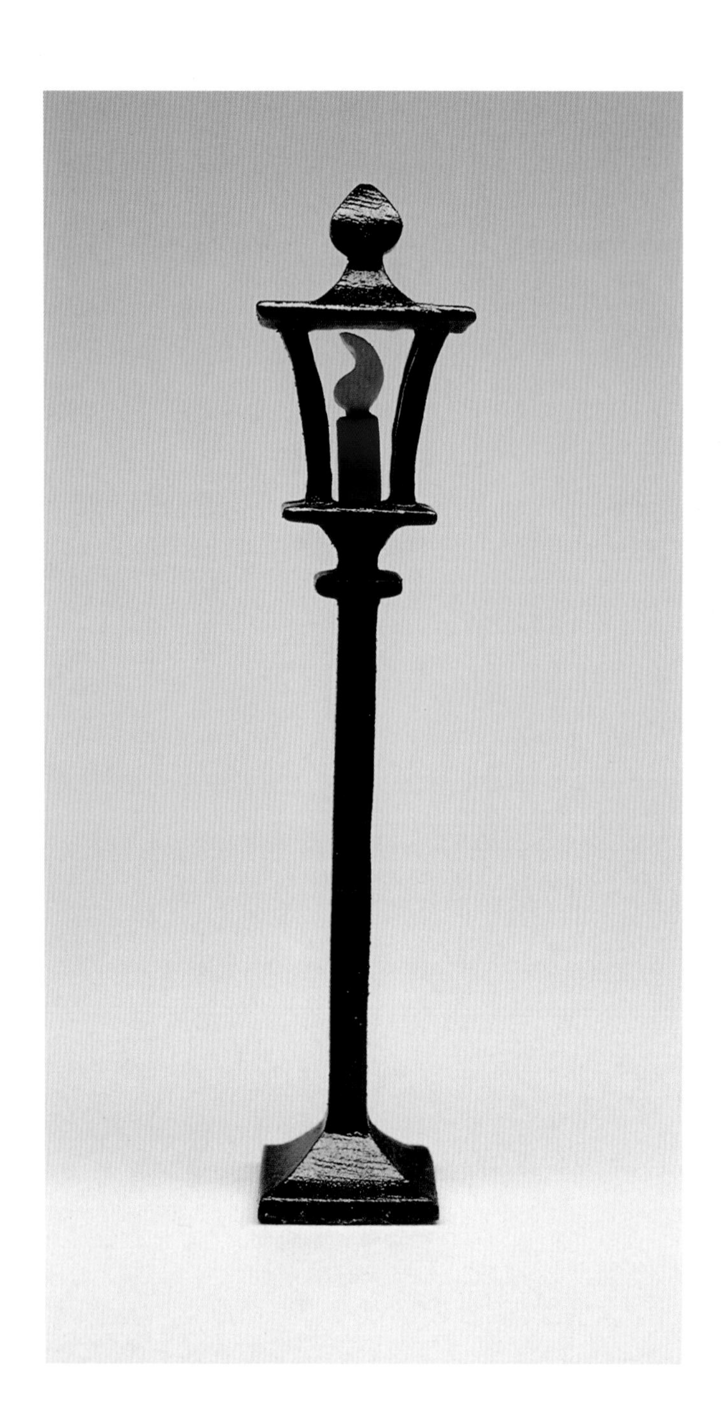

100%

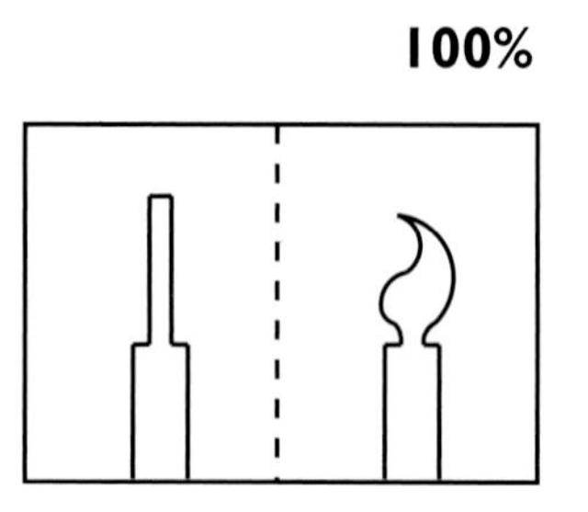

100%

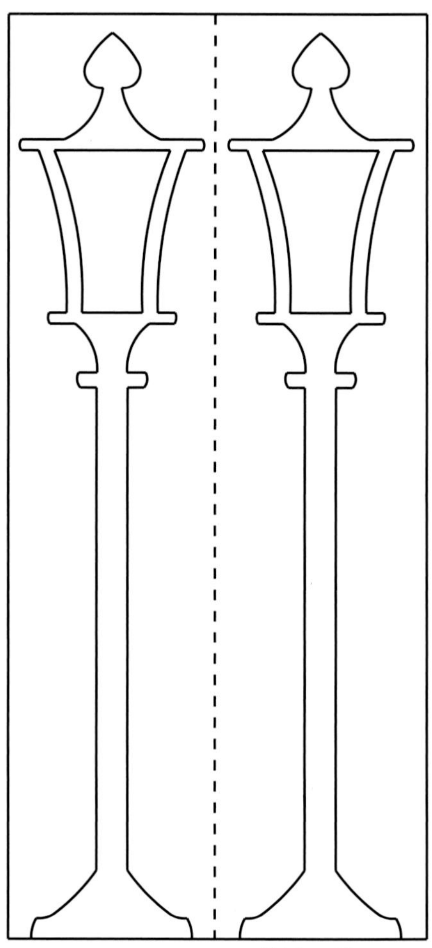

MANGER

100%

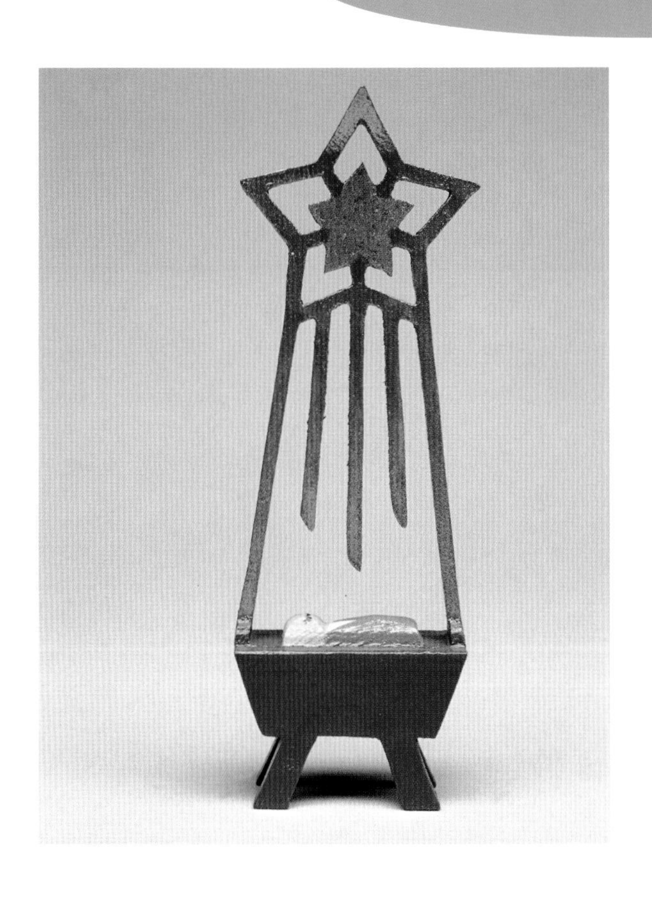

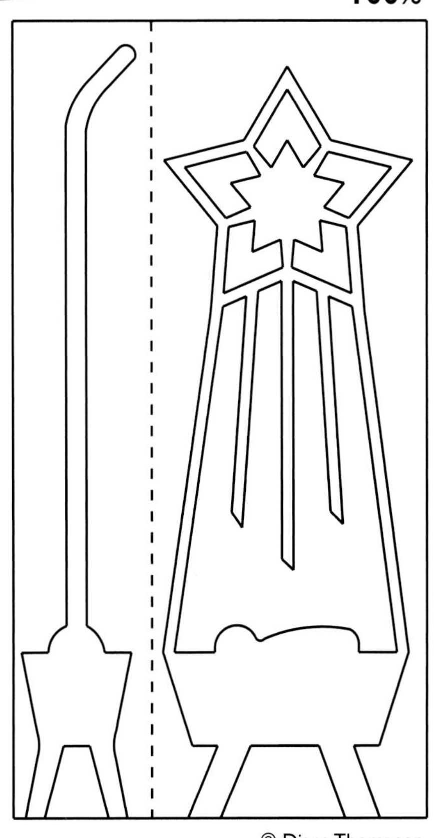

MR. WHISKERS

100%

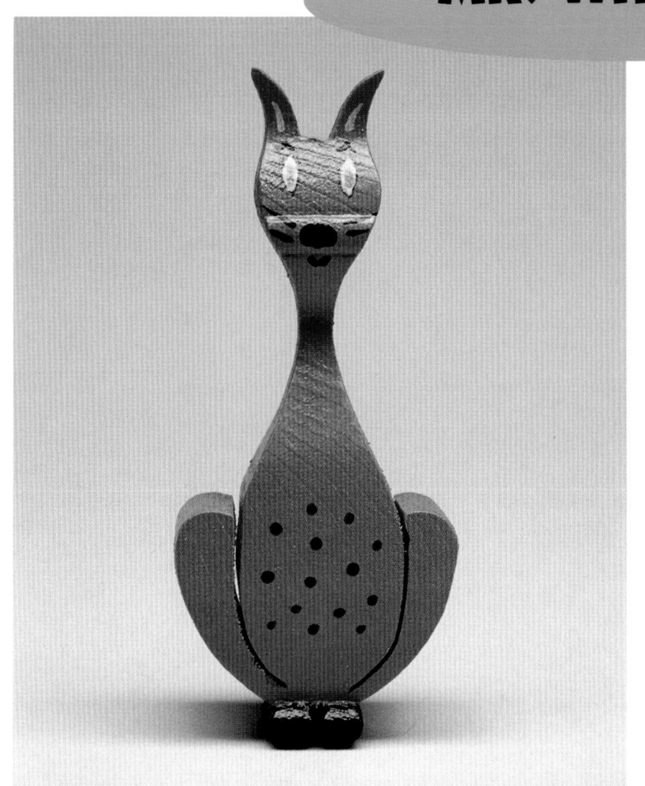

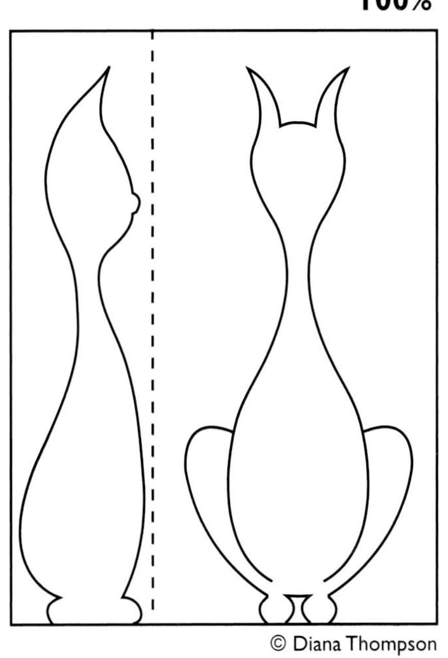

OLD RUGGED CROSS

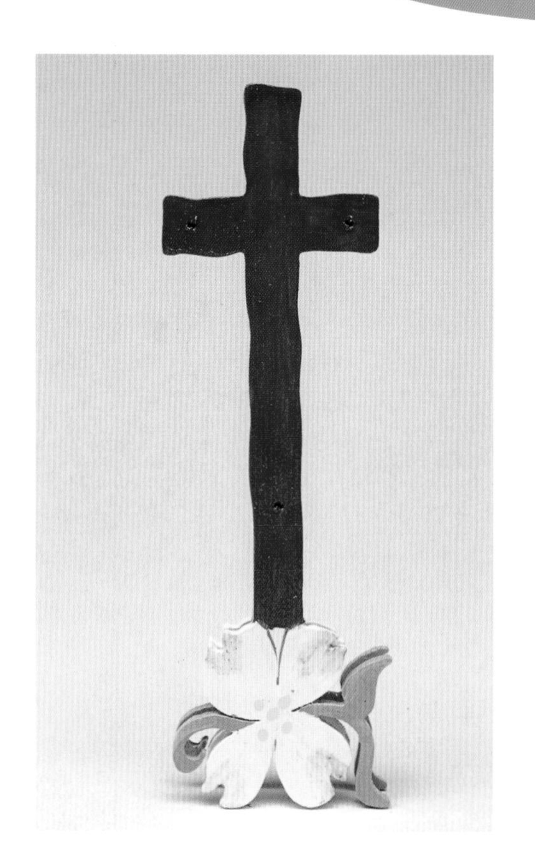

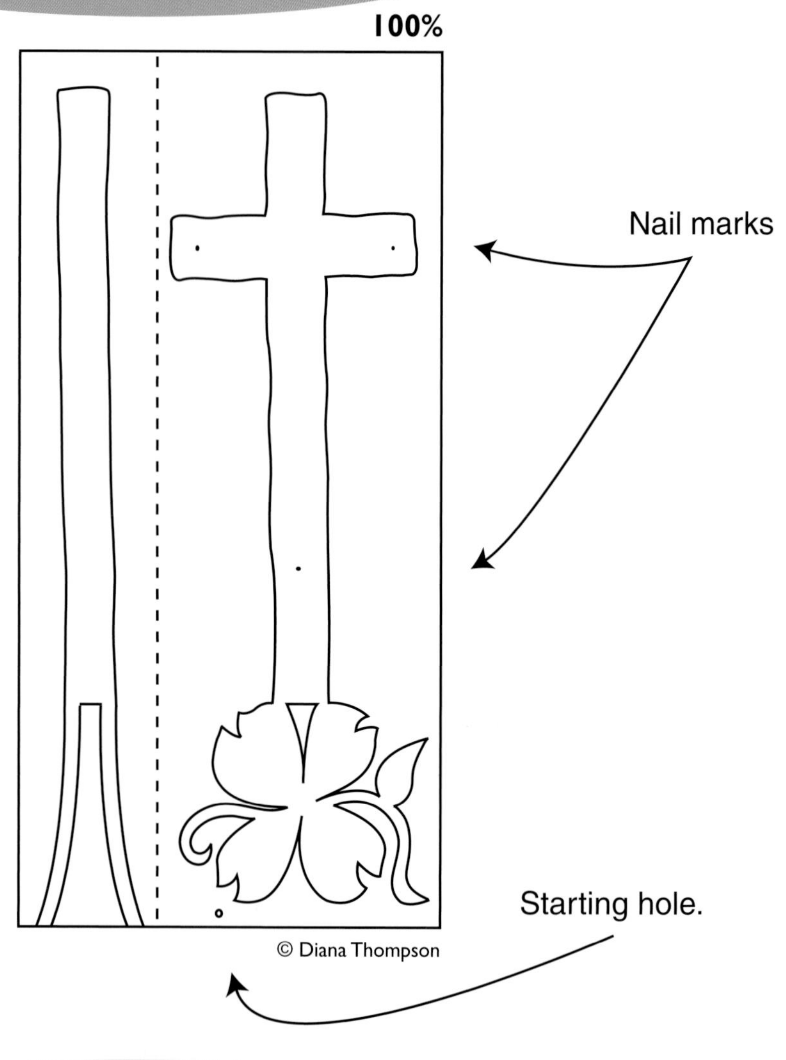

OLD SHOE

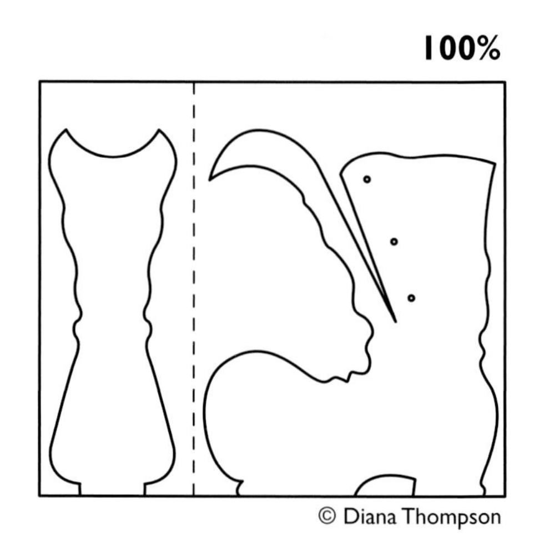

ORCA

100%

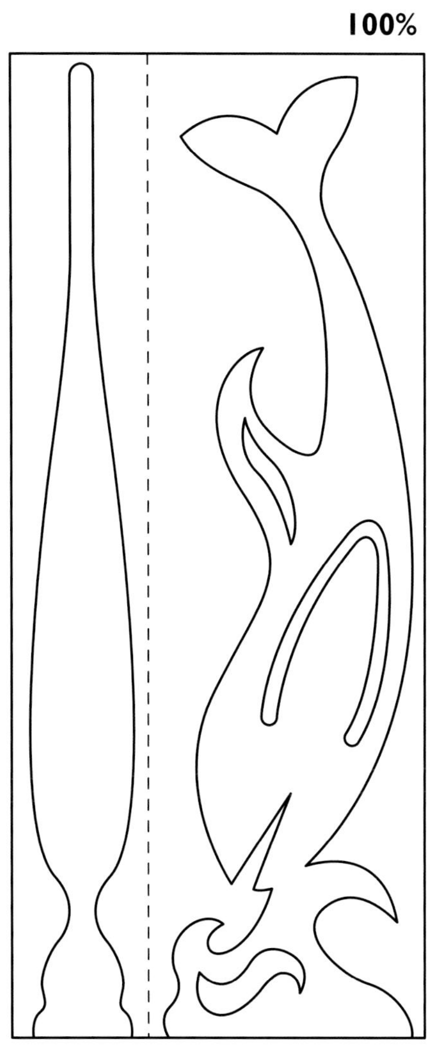

PELICAN

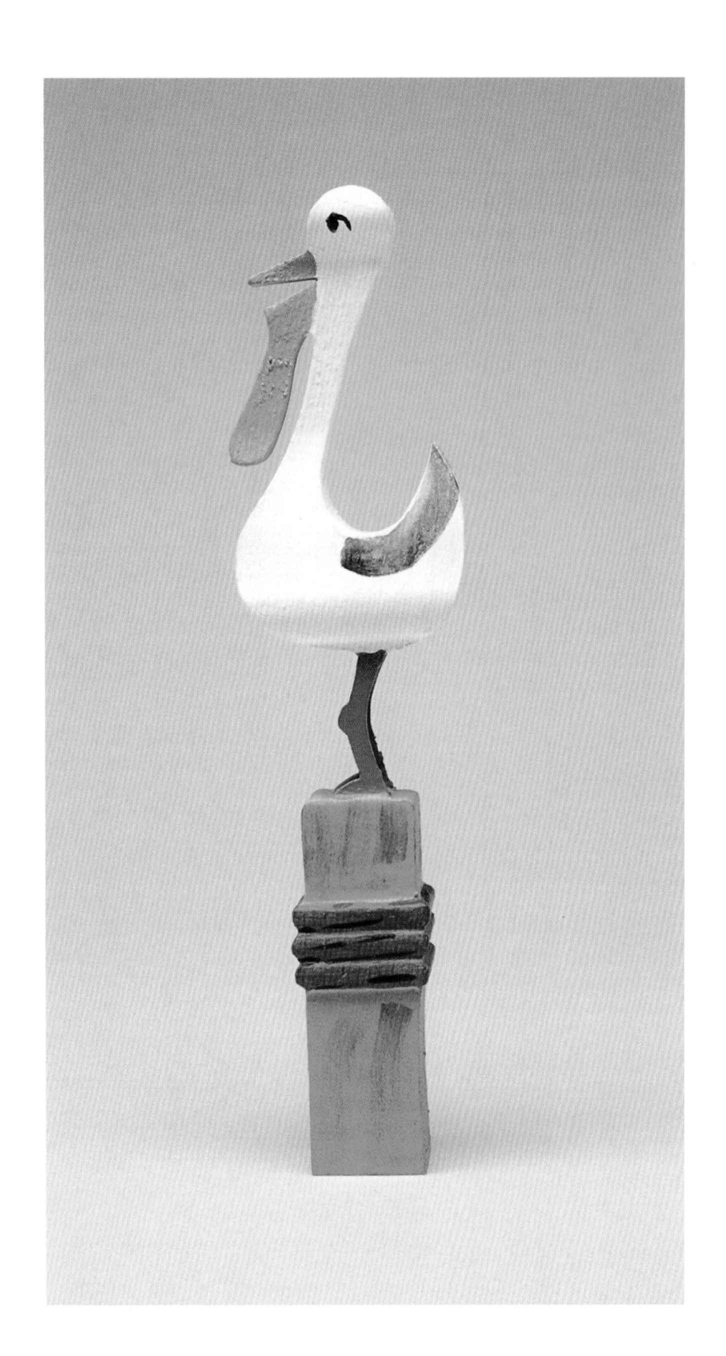

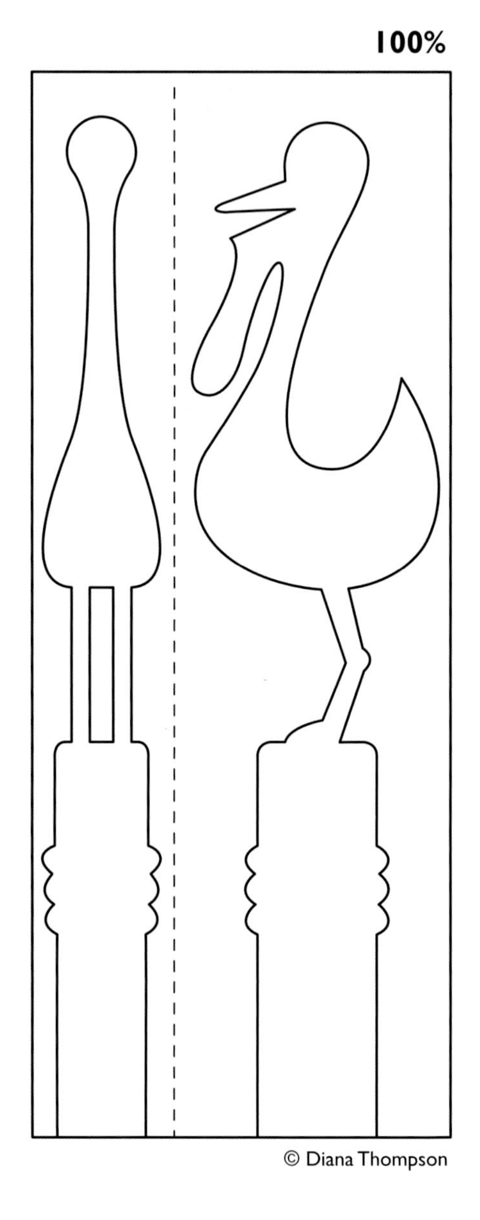

PENGUIN

100%

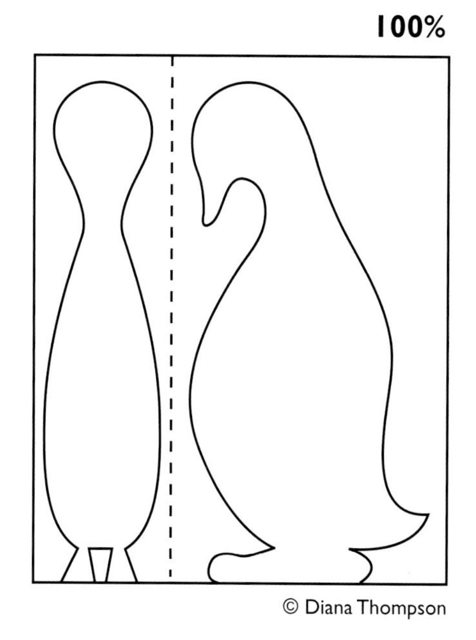

POT OF GOLD

100%

PUMPKIN

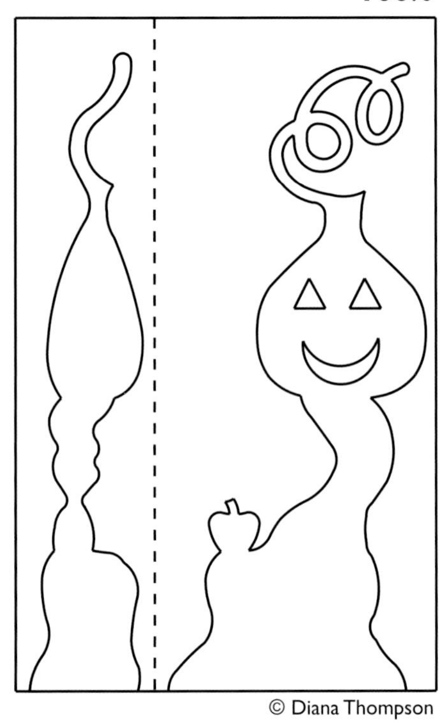

© Diana Thompson

ROB'S GOONY

100%

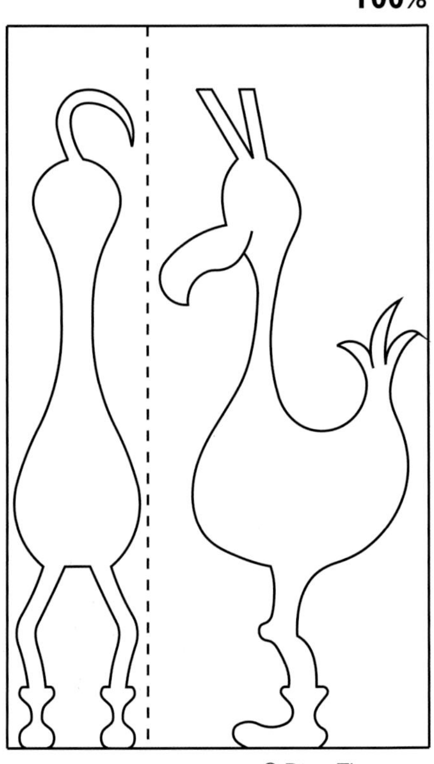

© Diana Thompson

SAILBOAT

100%

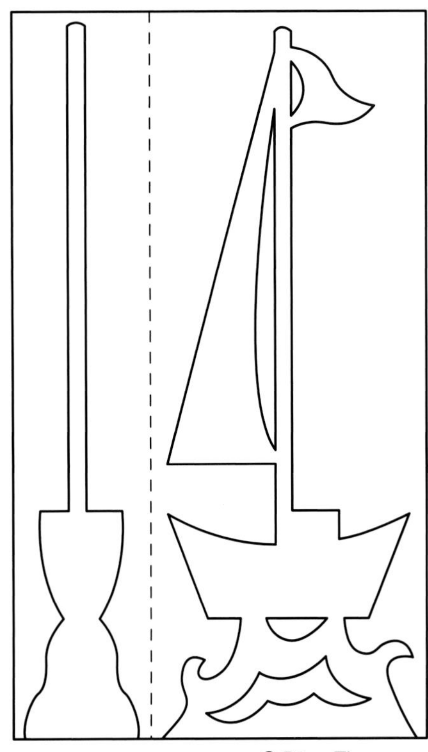

SNAIL

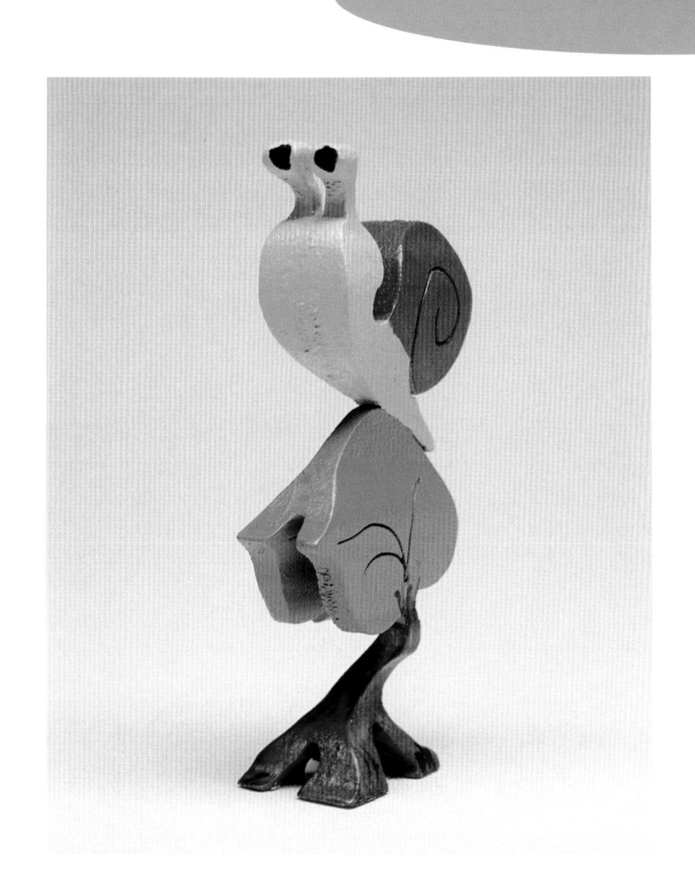

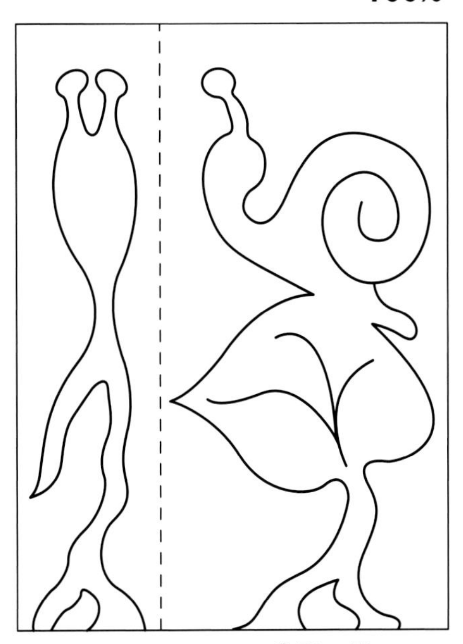

SNOWMAN

100%

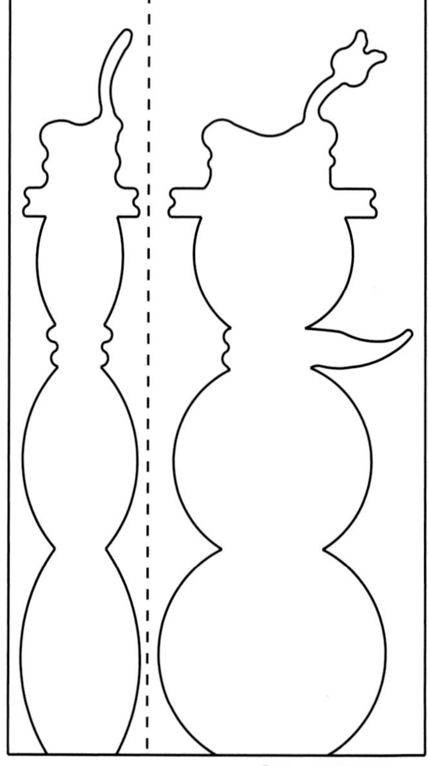

SONGBIRD

TEXAS

100%

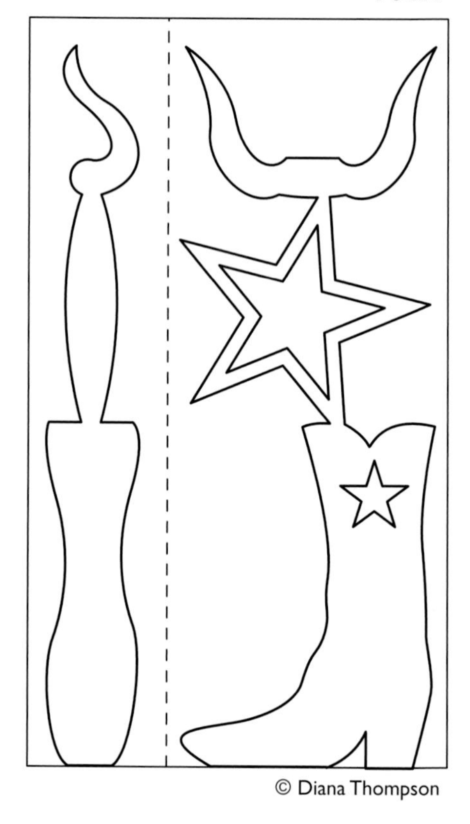

THANKFUL HANDS

100%

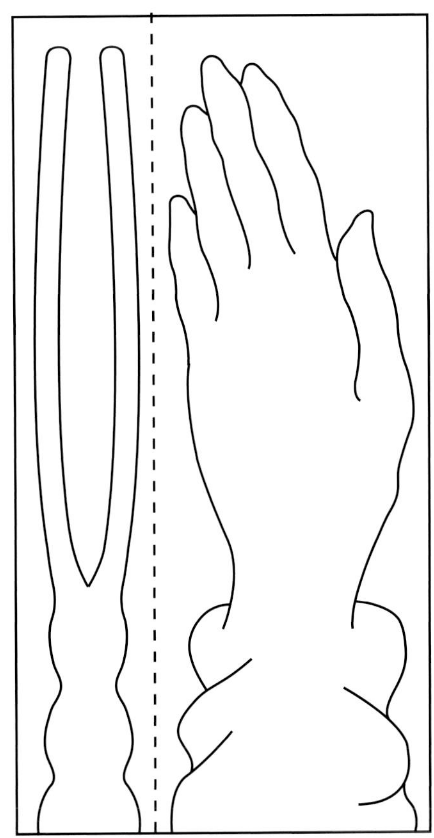

TRICK OR TREAT

100%

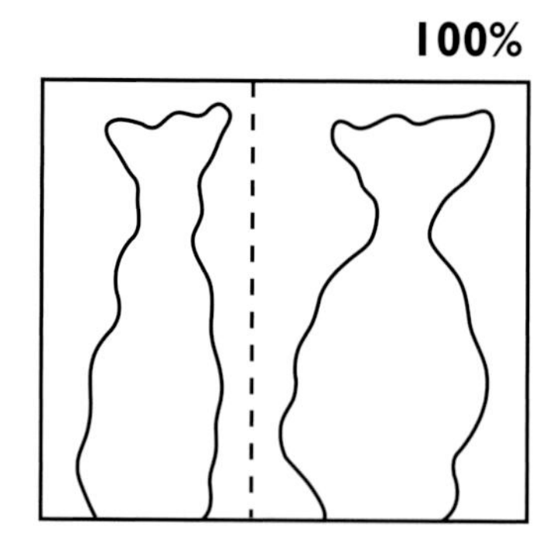

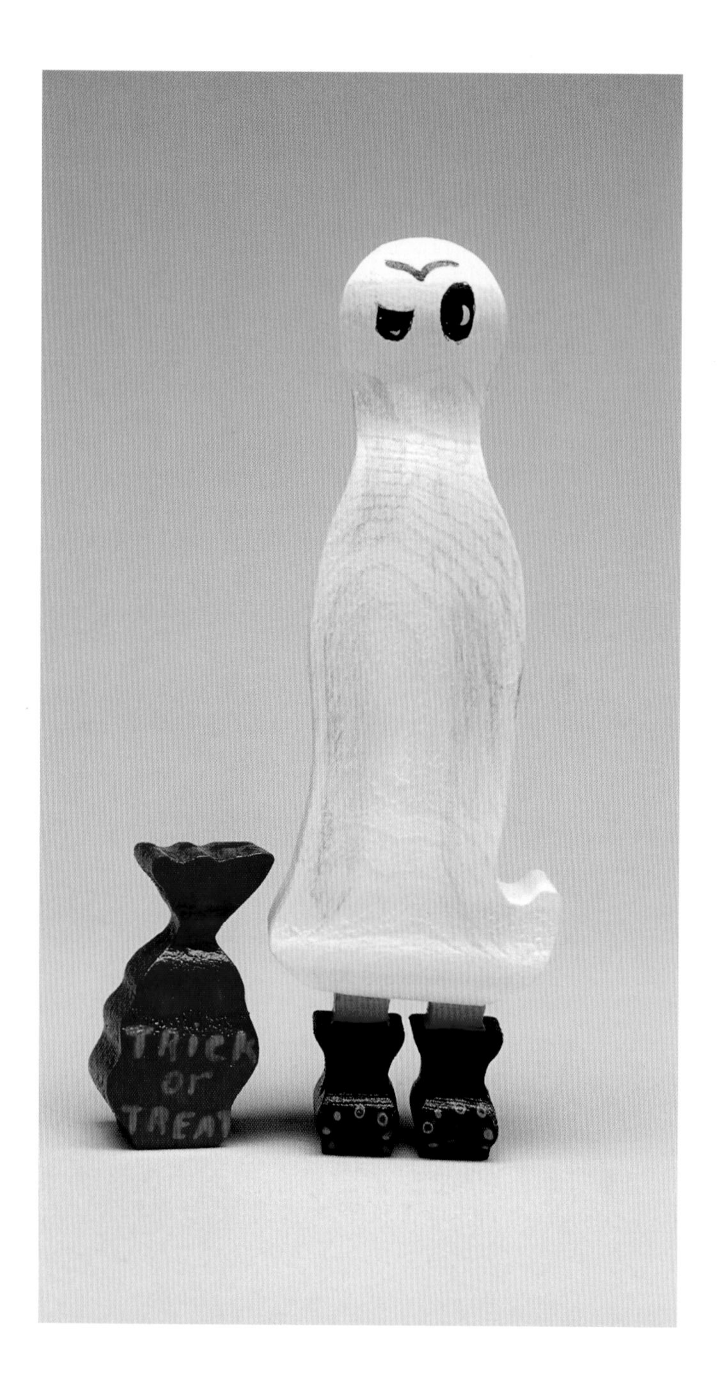

100%

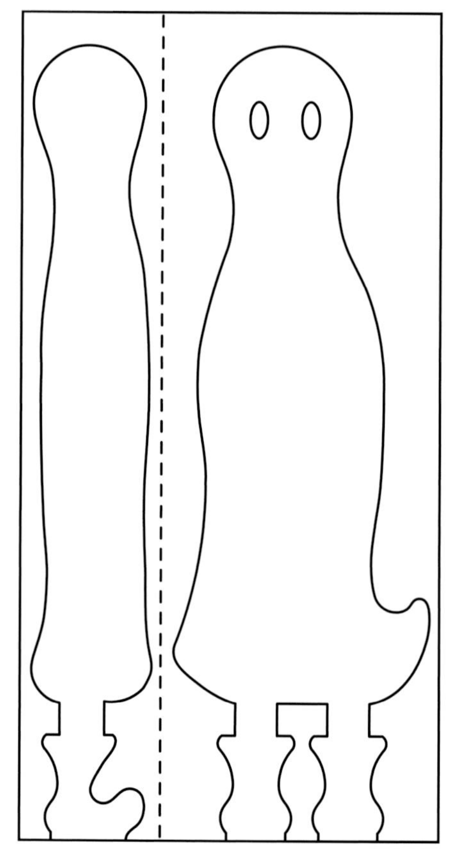

© Diana Thompson

TULIP

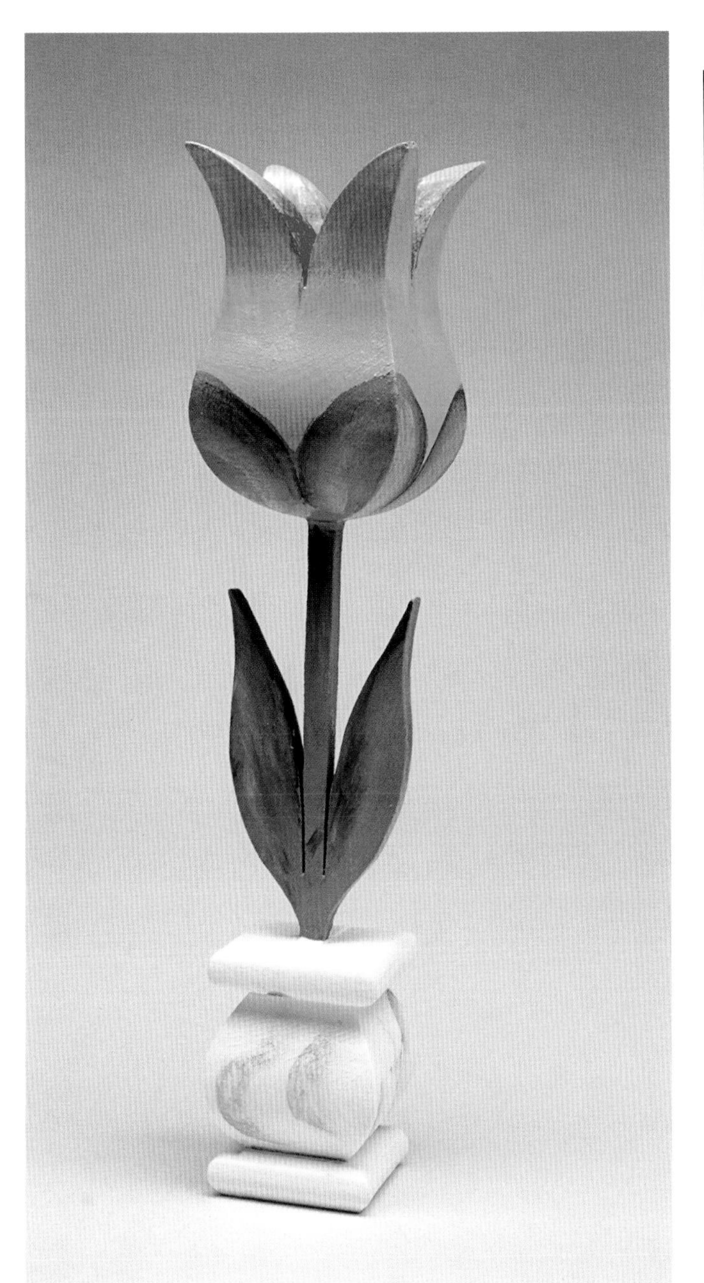

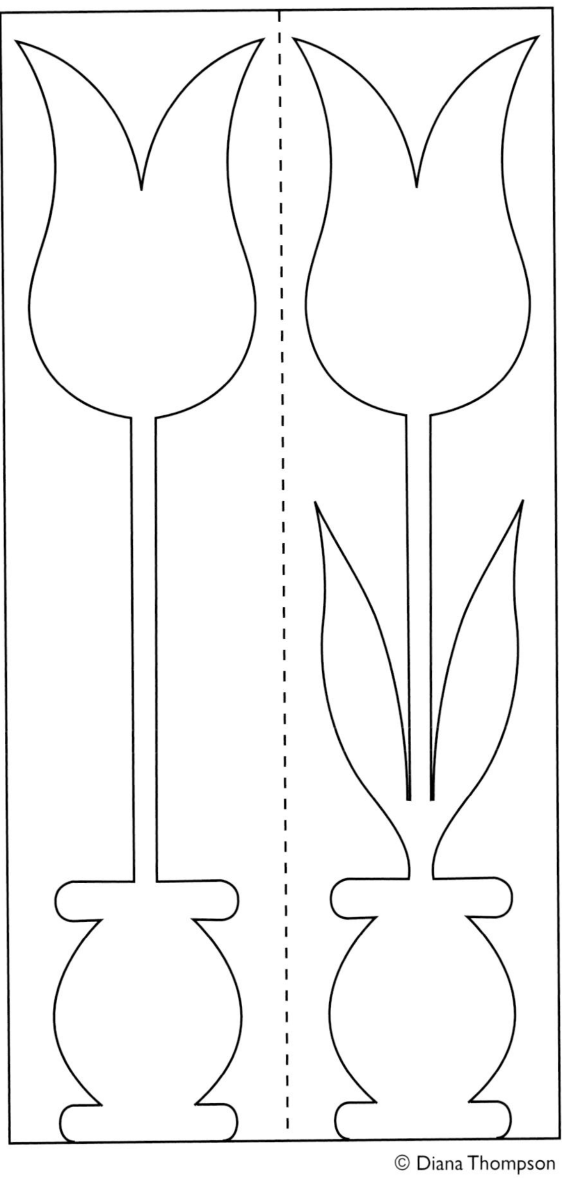

TURKEY

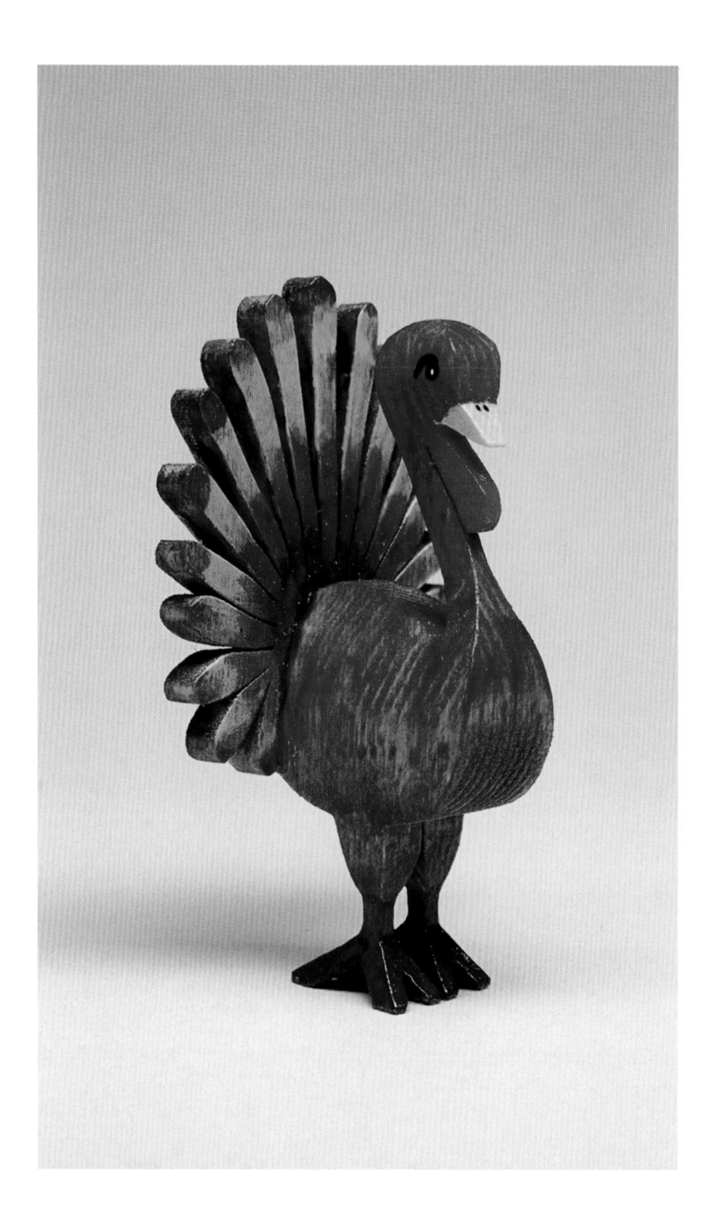

100%

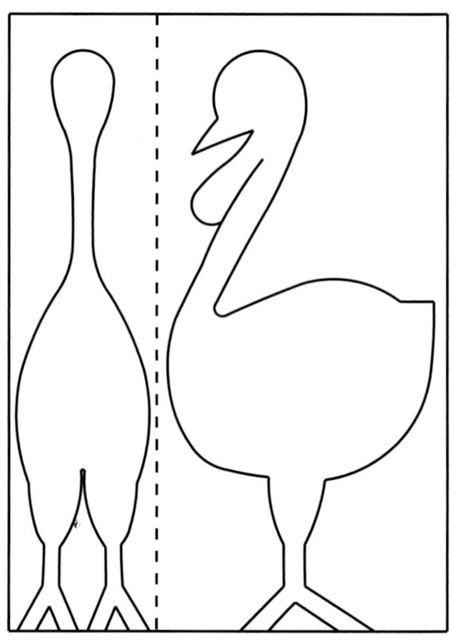

© Diana Thompson

100%

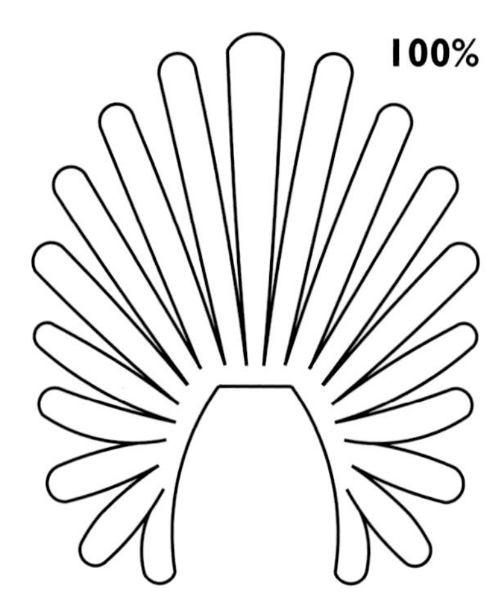

Note: Use thinner stock for the tail feathers.

GIRL & BOY VALENTINES

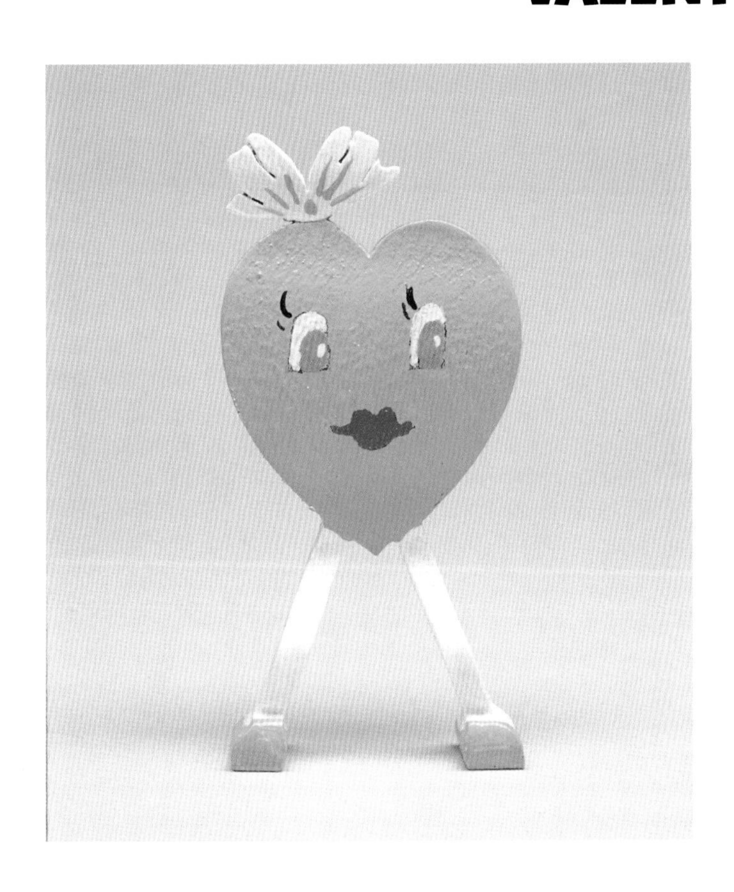

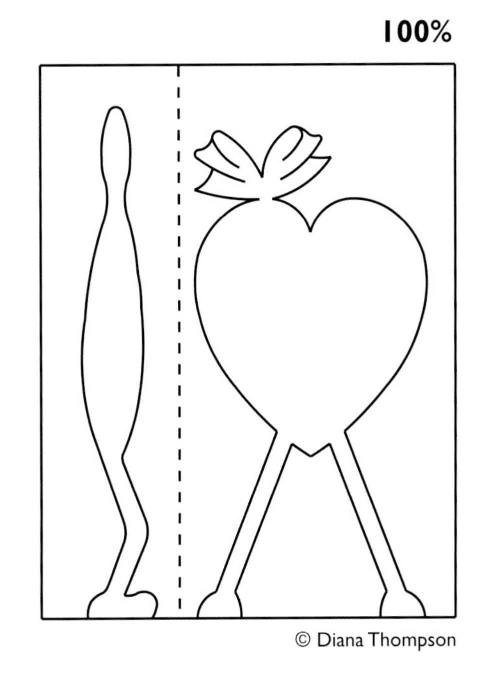

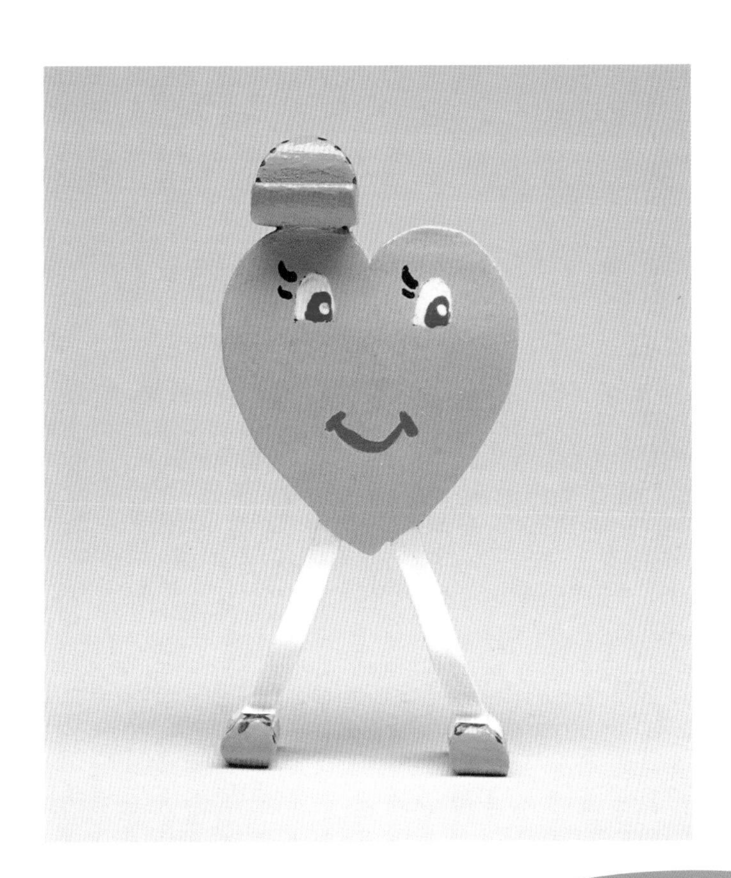

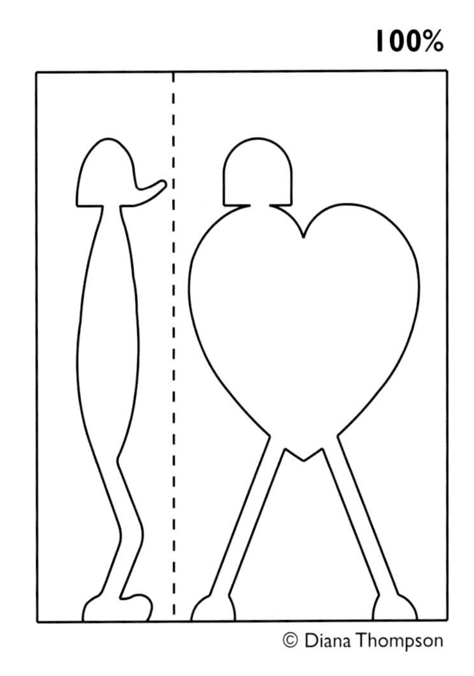

Swan and Seahorse Parade

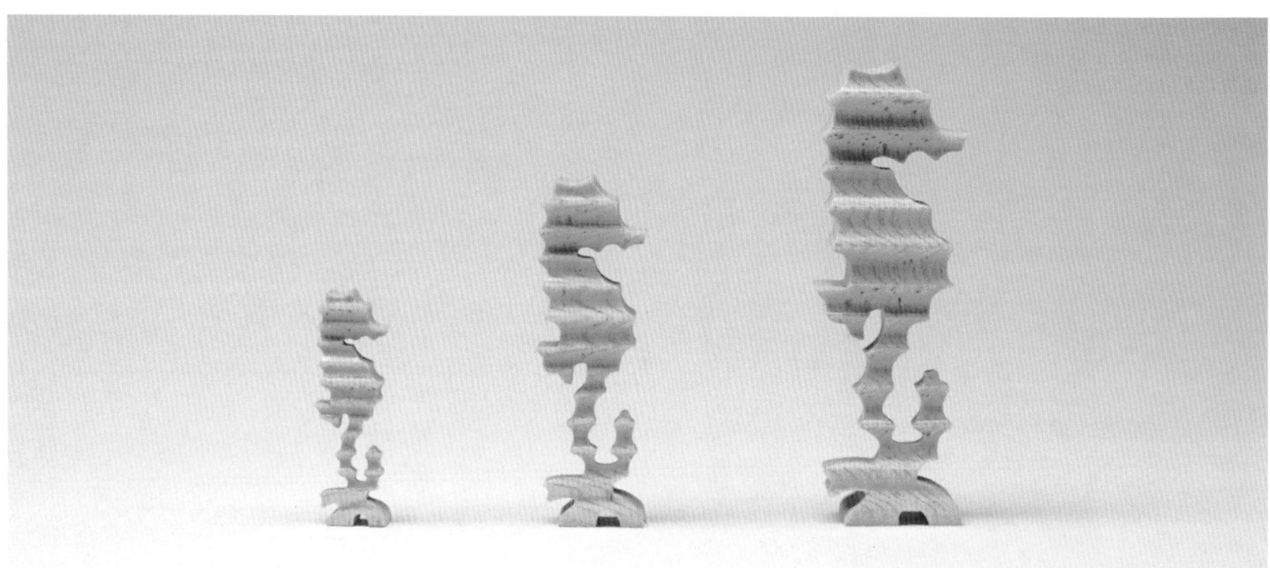

Any of the animal patterns in this book can be used in a "parade." Simply reduce the pattern in 25% increments. The patterns on the opposite page are shown at 100%, 75% and 50%. Other scales of reduction and enlargement will work as well.

PATTERN

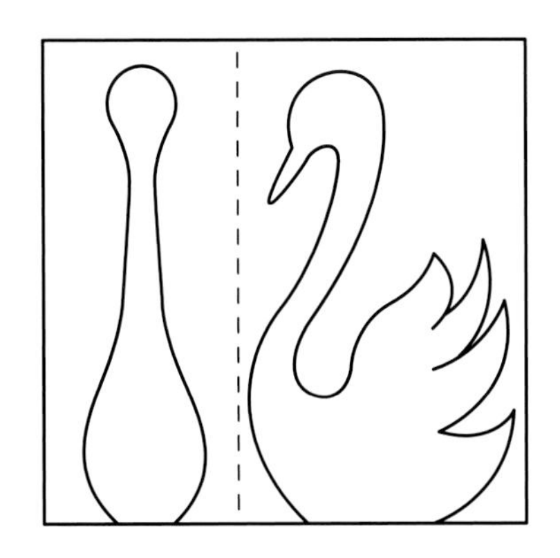

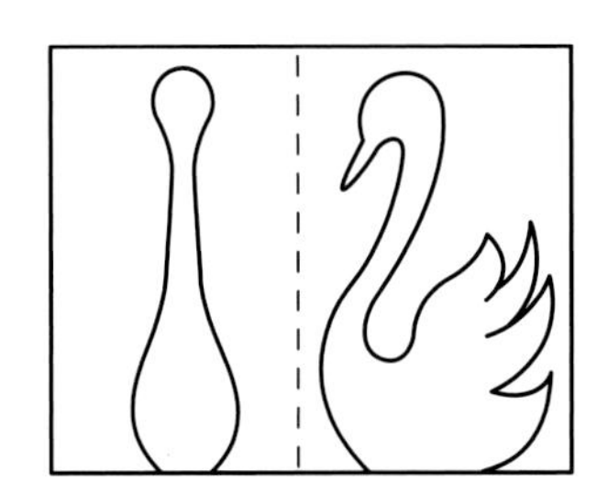

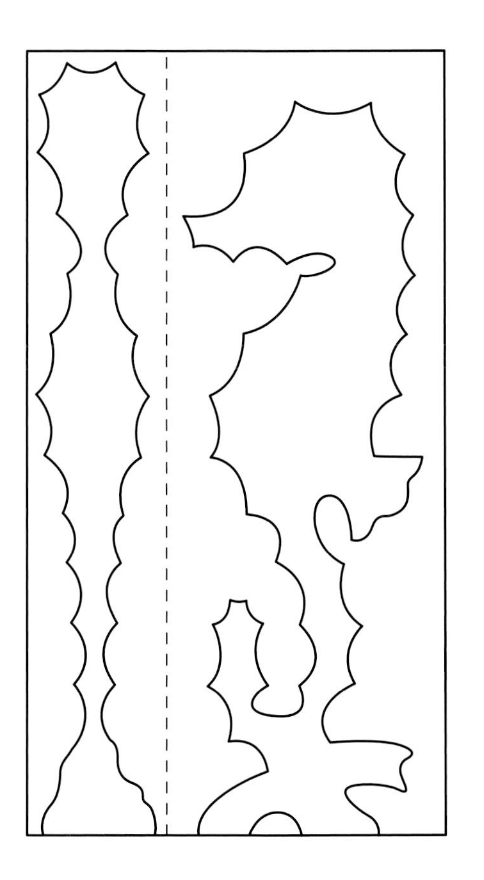

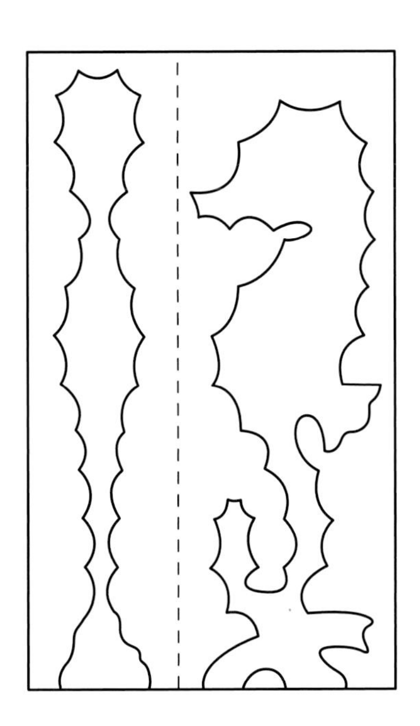

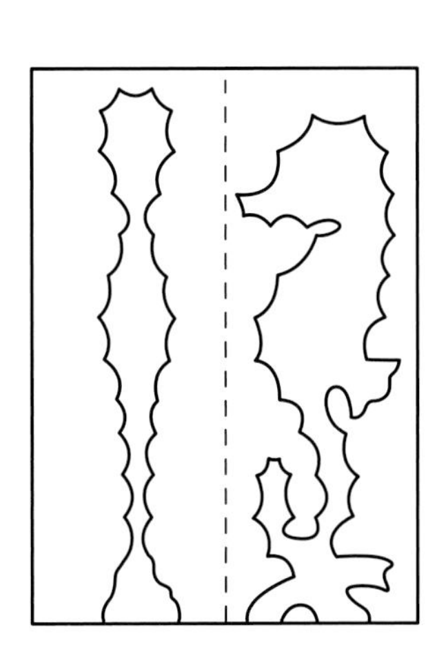

Use all patterns at 100%

Liberty Bell Project

This project makes an ideal display for Independence Day. The stand, the bell and the feet are cut separately and assembled to create a shiny, patriotic piece.

Supplies:

- $\frac{1}{4}$ in. by $3\frac{1}{2}$ in. by 5 in. stock of choice for the bell stand
- $\frac{3}{4}$ in. by $1\frac{1}{2}$ in. by $3\frac{1}{2}$ in. stock for the bell
- Brown thread to suspend the bell from the stand
- Needle
- Carpenters glue

PATTERN

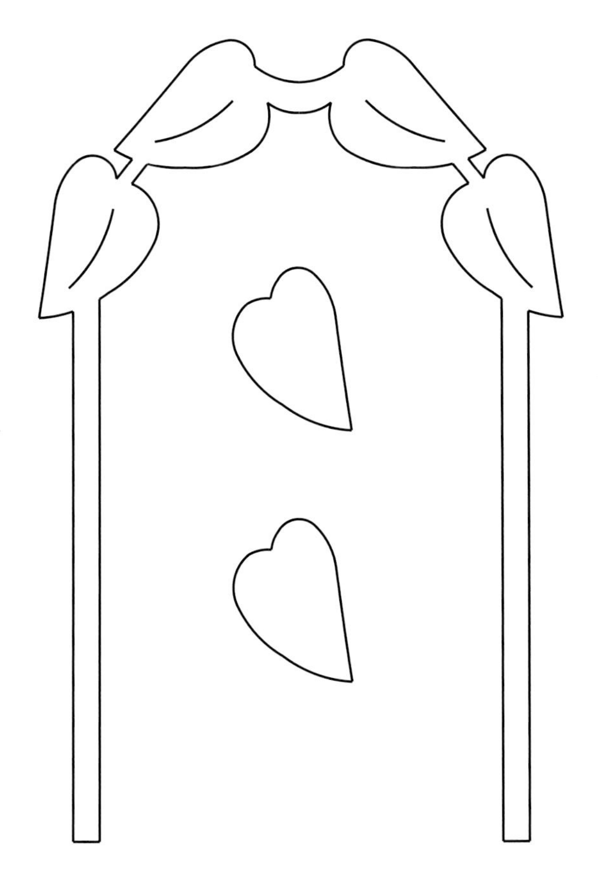

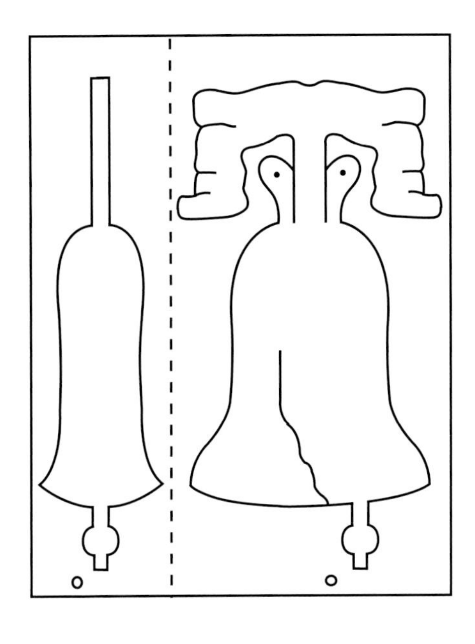

Apply the stand patterns to the stock, cut out the pieces and glue the feet to the legs of the stand.

Apply the bell pattern to the stock. Drill $^1/_{16}$ in. starter holes at the bottom of the pattern and two $^1/_{16}$ in. holes as marked to hang the bell. Thread the blade through the starter holes. Cut.

Apply the finish of your choice.

Using a double thread and needle, pull the thread through the bell holes and over the top of the stand. Tie a knot behind the stand and apply a small dab of glue to hold it in place.

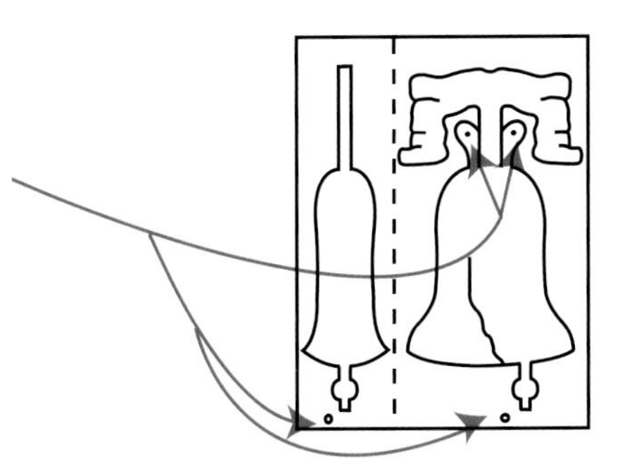

Use all patterns at 100%

Barnyard Project

Nothing beats a barnyard scene when it comes to displaying 3-D farm animals. Roosters, ducks, sheep, horses and goats are all part of this fun-to-scroll and fun-to-display project.

Cut the barn and the fence pieces according to the pattern. Cut the figures according to the general directions.

Following the diagram, glue the barn and the fence together with wood glue.

Seal all figures and the barn with a wood sealer of your choice. When the project is dry, lightly sand the piece with 220-grit sandpaper. Finish the barn and the animals with craft paints according to the photograph or as desired.

PATTERN

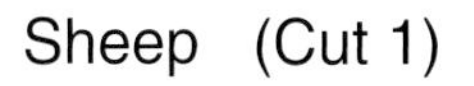
Sheep (Cut 1)

Horse (Cut 1)

Sheep (Cut 1)

Rooster (Cut 1)

Hen (Cut 2)

Rooster (Cut 1)

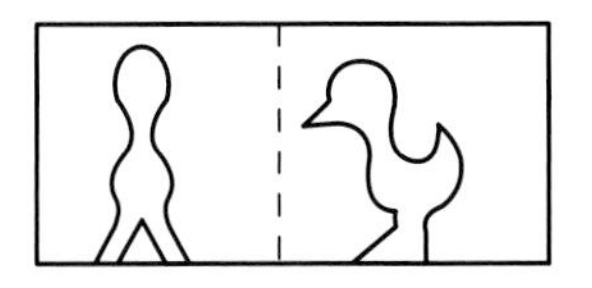

Baby chick (Cut 3)

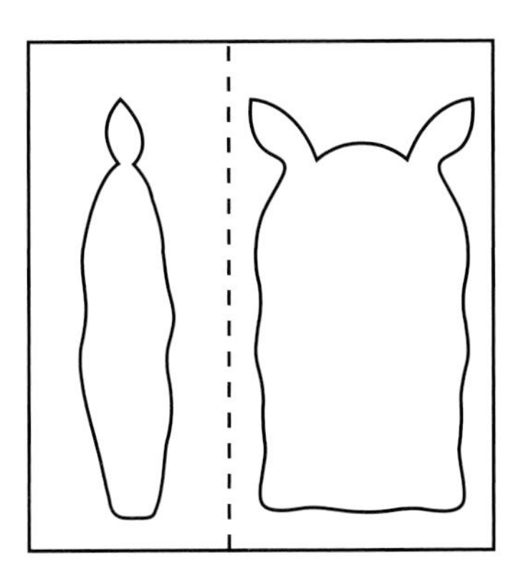

Feedbag (Cut 2)

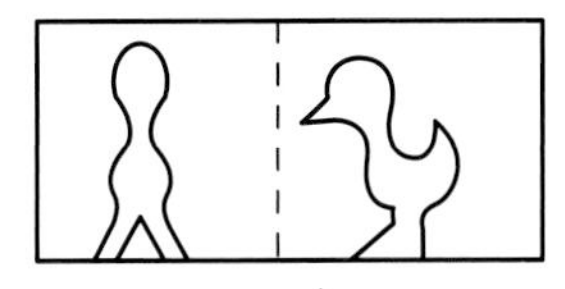

Baby chick (Cut 3)

Use all patterns at 100%

PATTERN

Sides and stall seperations

(Cut 5)

Roof Center
(Cut 2)

Center - Bevel 15 degrees

Side - Bevel 13 1/2 degrees

Roof side
(Cut 2)

Side - Bevel 13 1/2 degrees

End - Bevel 45 degrees

Use 1/4" stock for all barn pieces and fence parts.

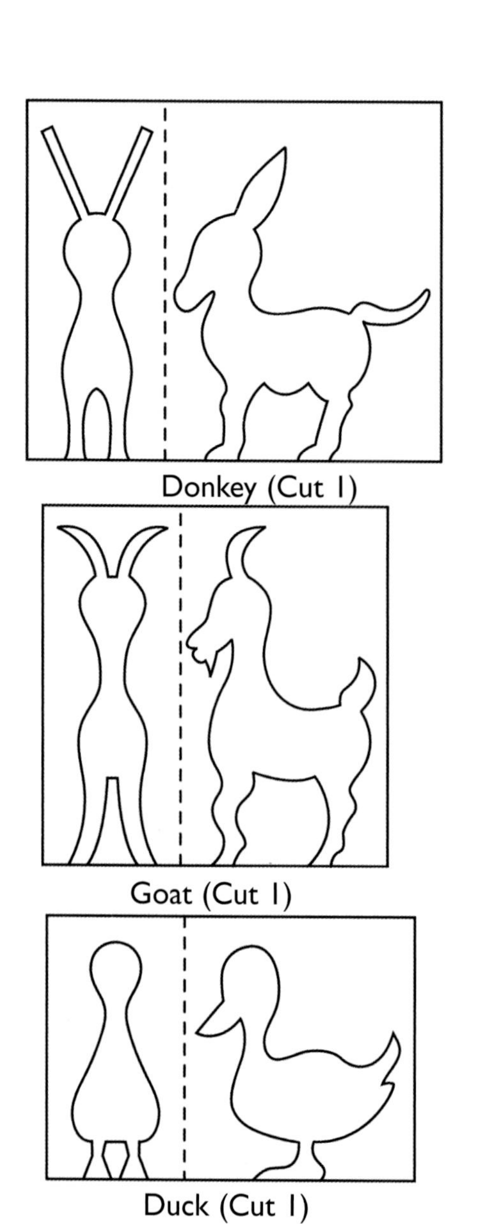
Donkey (Cut 1)

Goat (Cut 1)

Duck (Cut 1)

Use all patterns at 100%

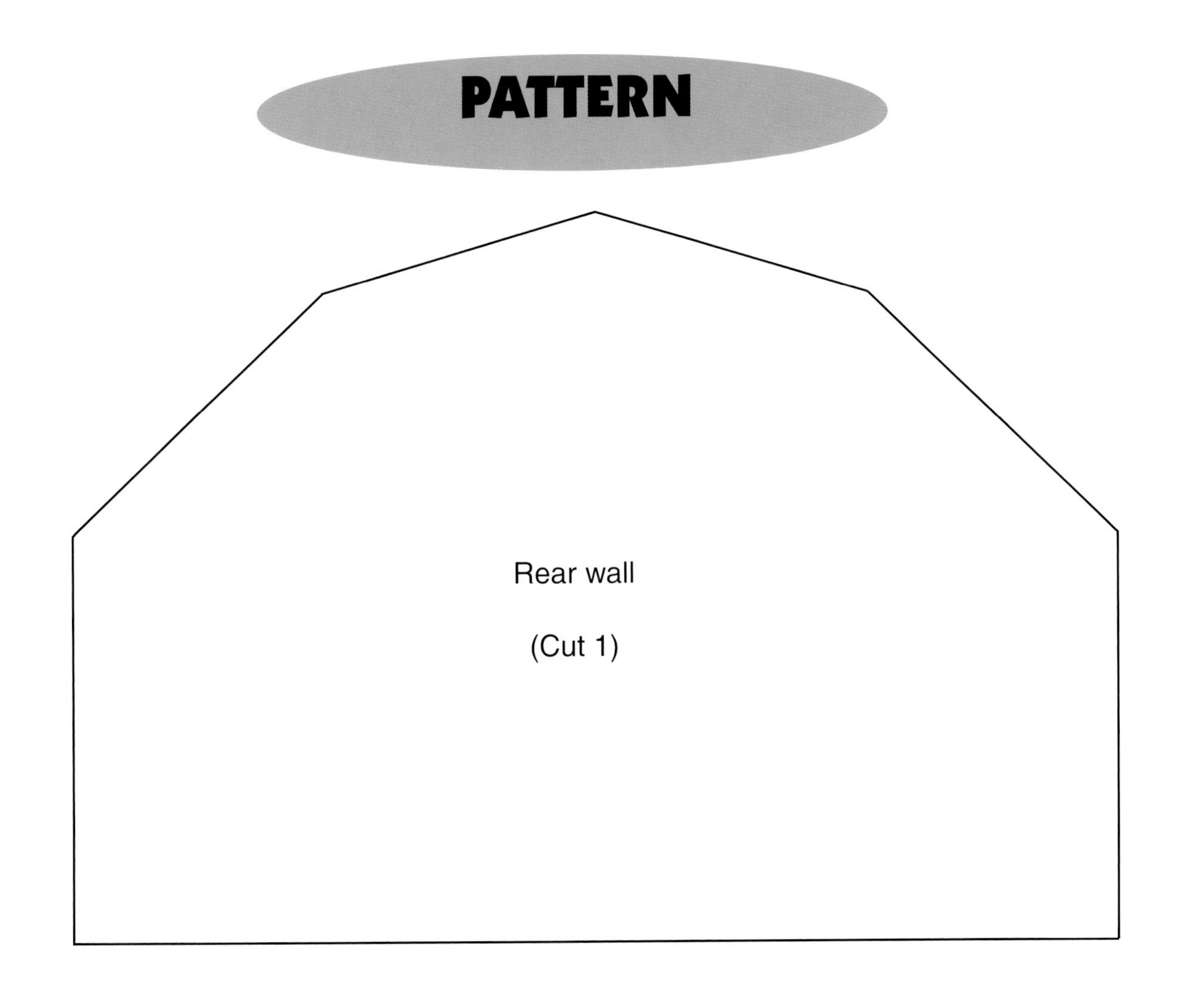

Fence

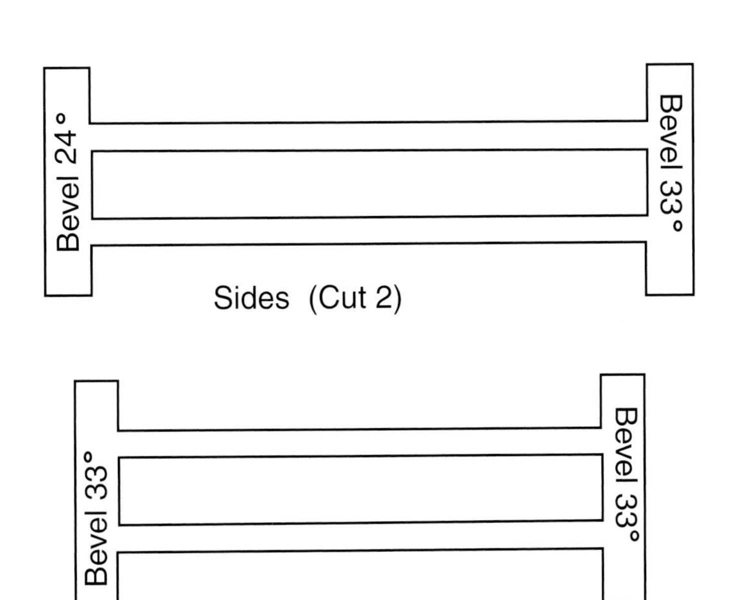

Use all patterns at 100%

Assembly Guide

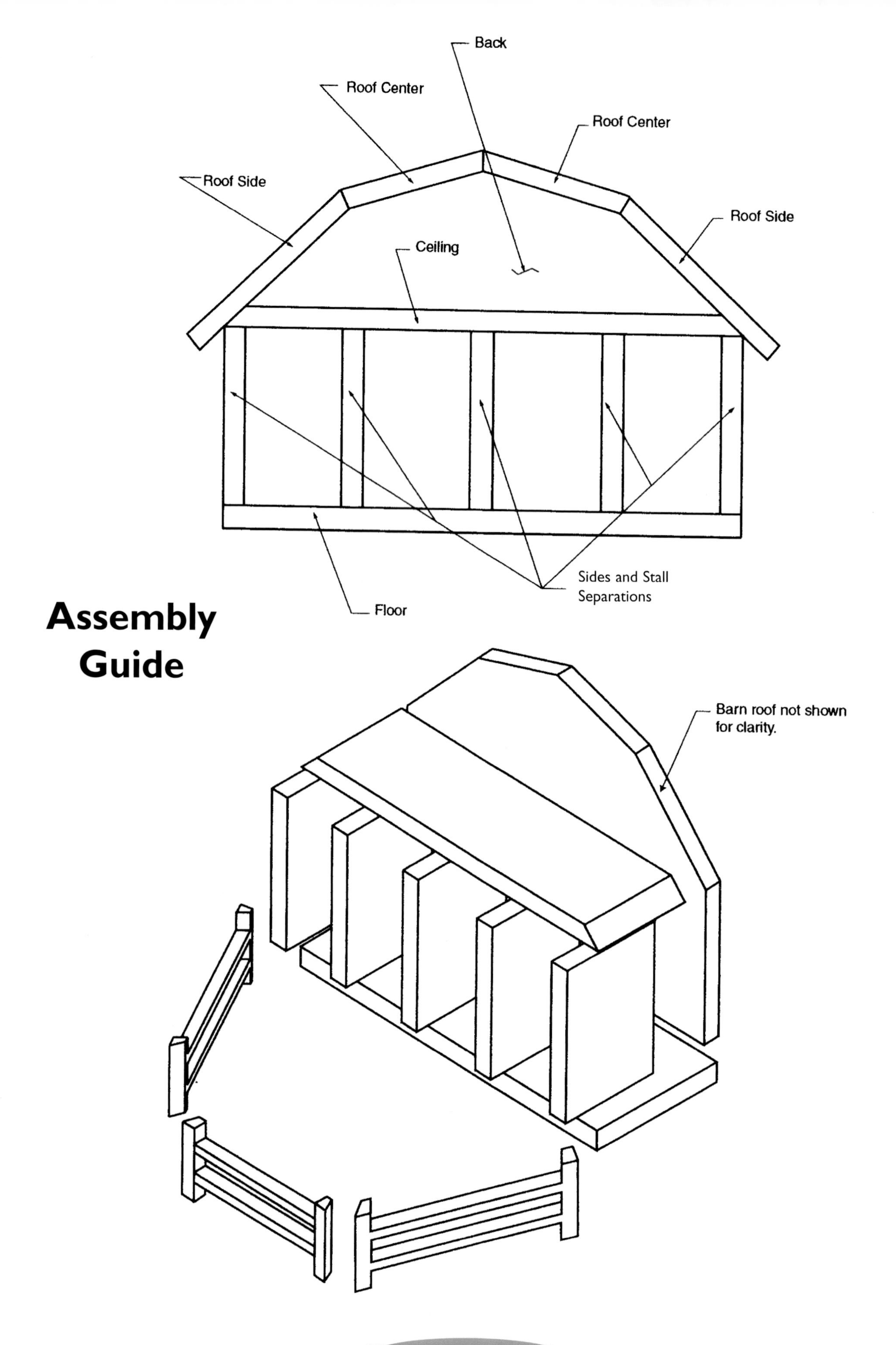

Mr. and Mrs. Santa Music Box Project

Make the holidays even more special with this Santa music box. The figures are cut separately and glued in the base to create a festive Christmas scene.

Supplies:

- Musical movement
- Decorative snow
- White glue
- (3) No. 2 by 3/8 in. round head screws
- (2) No. 2 by 1/2 in. round or flat screws
- Small screw driver

Assemble the four sides of the music box base with wood glue. Remove the cover of the musical movement and attach it to the underside of the top with screws. Make sure the shaft is visible through the center hole. Replace the cover and glue the box top assembly to the side assembly, flush with the top.

Note: The top fit is dependent on the thickness of the wood used for the sides. Not all 1/4-inch wood is uniform. I would suggest, after the sides have been assembled, that you trace around the inside to make your own top pattern. This way, you are assured of a good fit.

Attach the revolving platform to the underside of the large platform with the three #2 by 3/8 in. screws. It helps to pre-drill the holes first with a 1/16 in. drill bit.

Cut out the presents, book and cat using the trapping method as described on page 7. Cut the bodies of Mr. Santa and Mrs. Santa and the tree.

The arms are a triple cut. See the pattern for the order of the cuts. Use plenty of tape after each cut to hold the arms in the block until all the cuts are complete.

For the chairs, cut the frets from the right side of the pattern first and save them for future use. Cut the frets from the left side and discard them. Using the trapping method, finish cutting the pattern according to the general directions, returning the frets to the right side before making the final cut. This helps to hold the figure more steadily in the block. Note: The rocking chairs will not stand by themselves because of the curve at the top, but they will sit up just fine once the figures are glued into them.

Glue the arms on Mr. and Mrs. Santa. Coat all surfaces with a wood sealer of choice. After drying, sand gently with 220-grit sandpaper.

Finish the figures according to the photograph or with colors of your choice. When dry, spray the figures with a clear finish. I've found the snow stays whiter if it is applied after the clear finish.

Using the white glue, glue Mr. and Mrs. Santa into their rocking chairs. Glue the book into his lap and the small present into hers. Glue all the figures to the top platform according to the photo or as desired. Set the platform on top of a bowl during this step to hold them steady and upright while you work.

Center the shaft through the hole in the box assembly and screw it into place. Turn the platform to wind the musical movement.

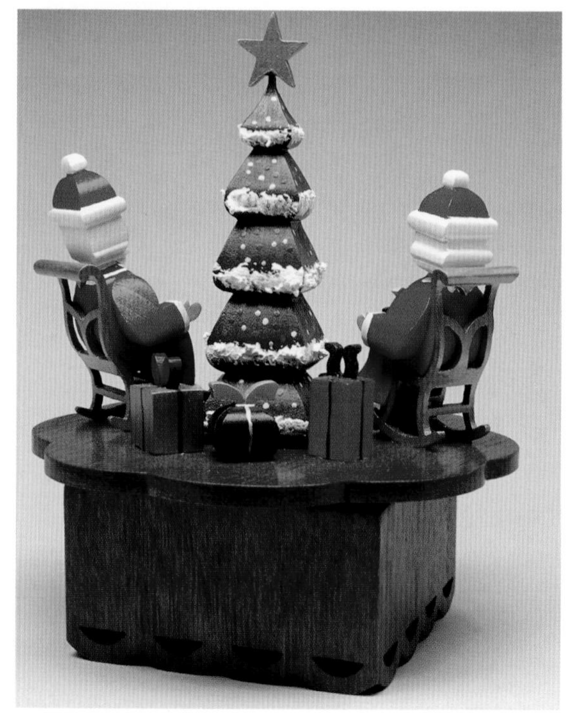

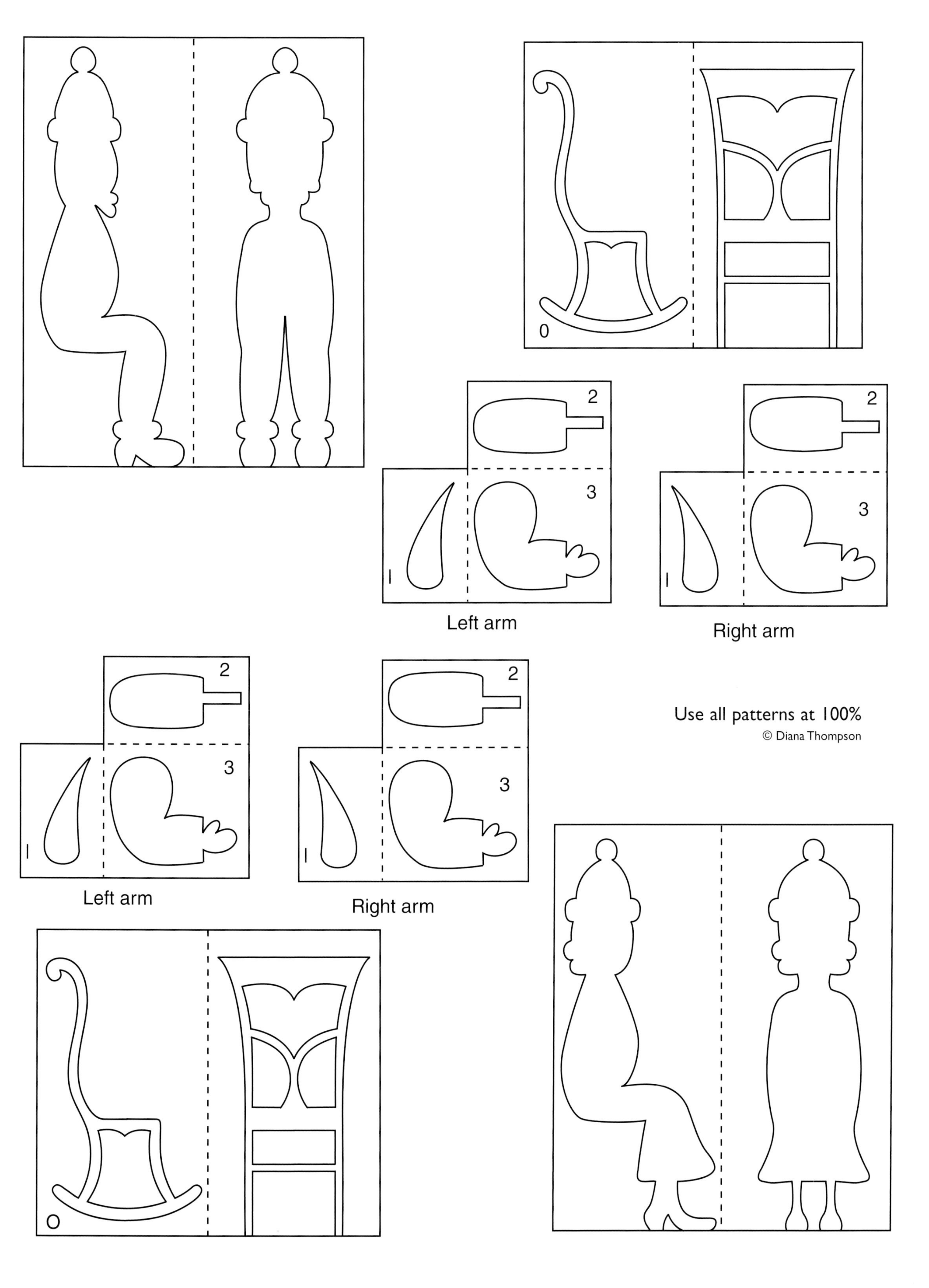
0
2
3
1
Left arm
2
3
1
Right arm
2
3
1
Left arm
2
3
1
Right arm
0
Use all patterns at 100%

PATTERN

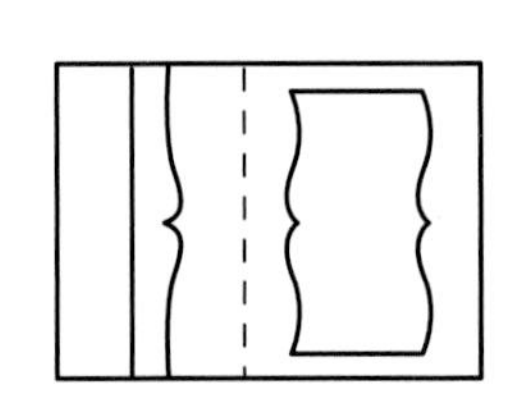

Use all patterns at 100%

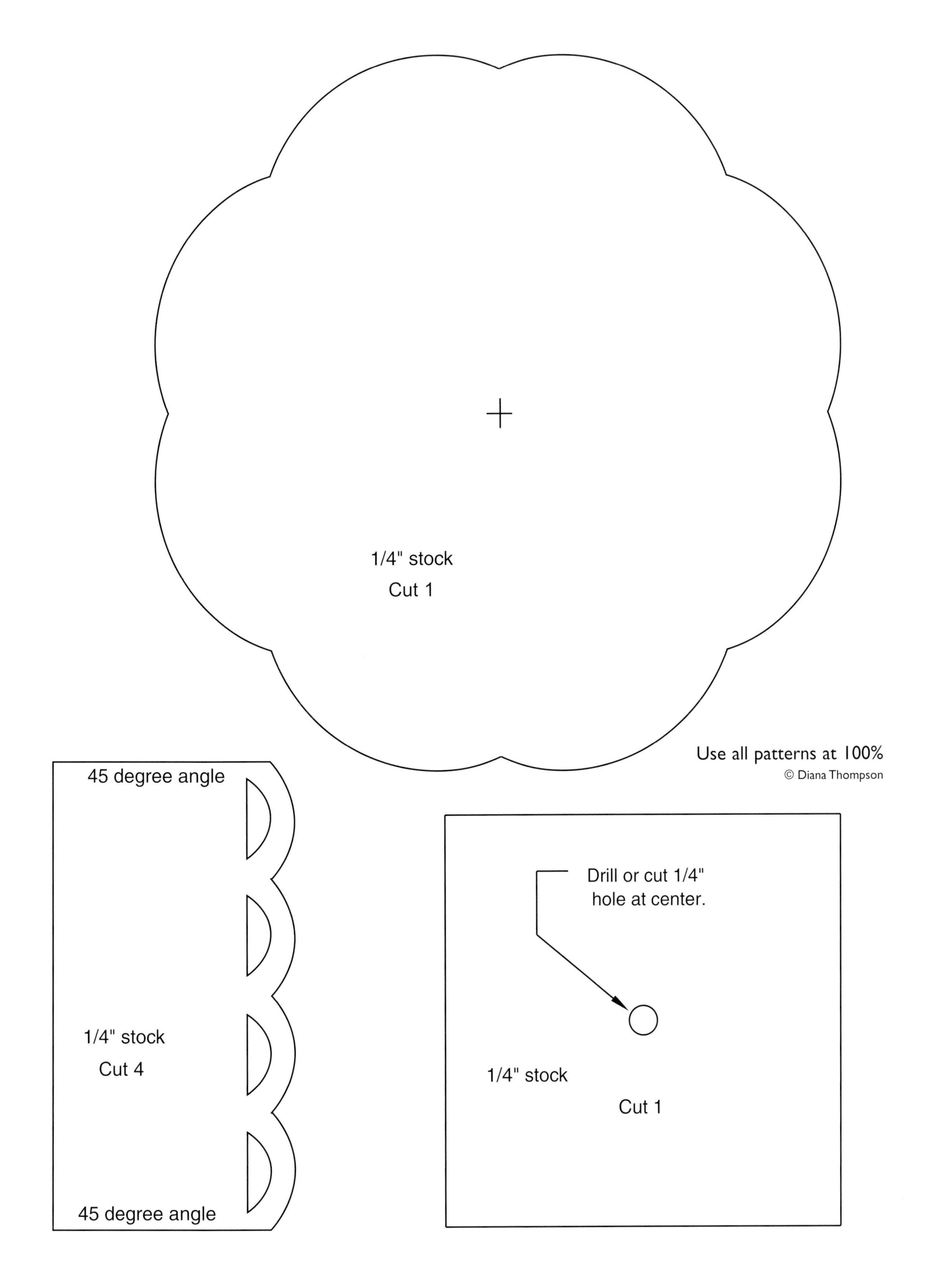
1/4" stock
Cut 1
Use all patterns at 100%
© Diana Thompson
45 degree angle
1/4" stock
Cut 4
45 degree angle
Drill or cut 1/4"
hole at center.
1/4" stock
Cut 1

Assembly Guide

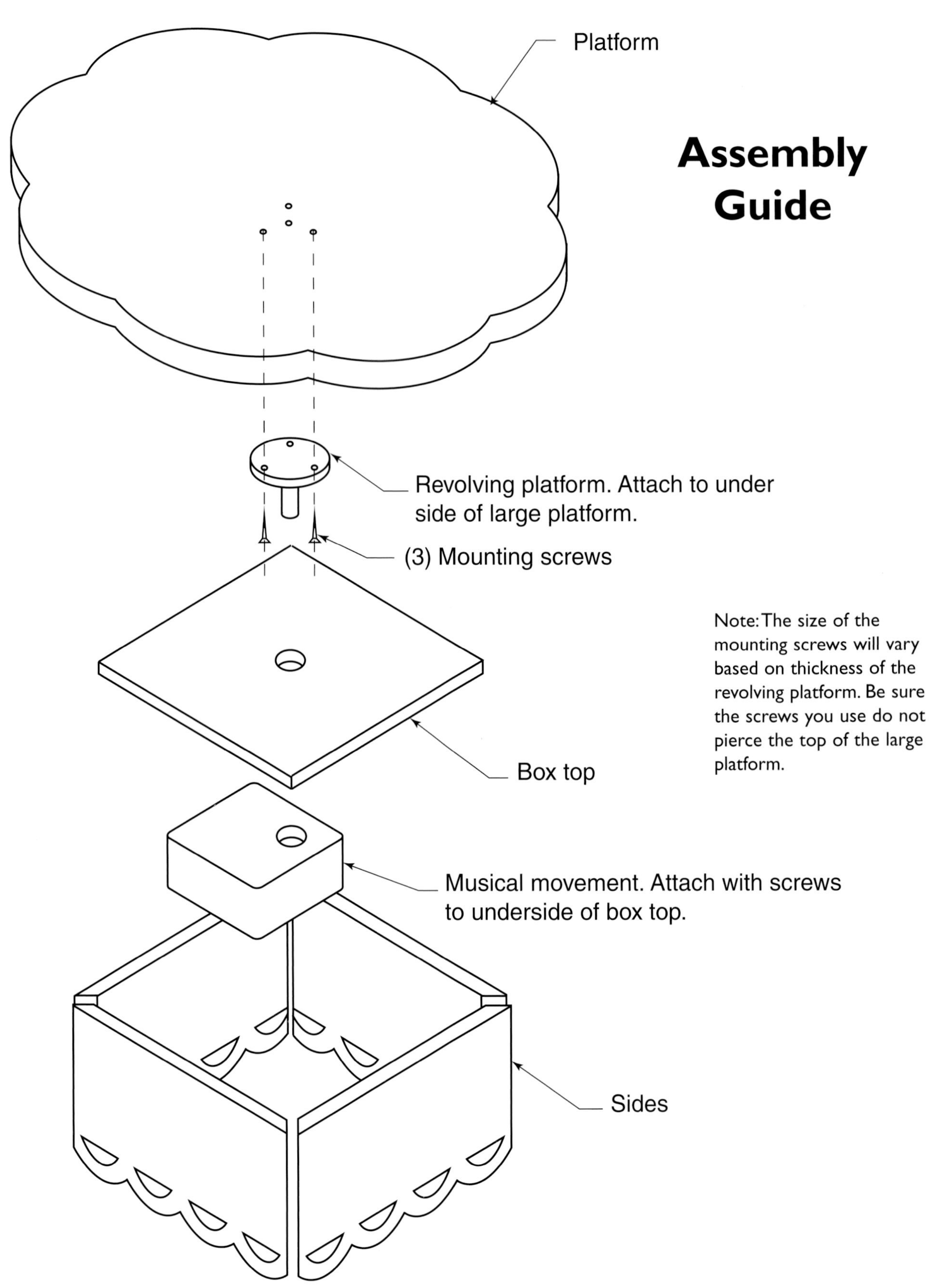

Note: The size of the mounting screws will vary based on thickness of the revolving platform. Be sure the screws you use do not pierce the top of the large platform.

Scroll Saw WorkShop

The How-To Magazine for Scrollers

Don't Miss A Single Issue Subscribe Today!

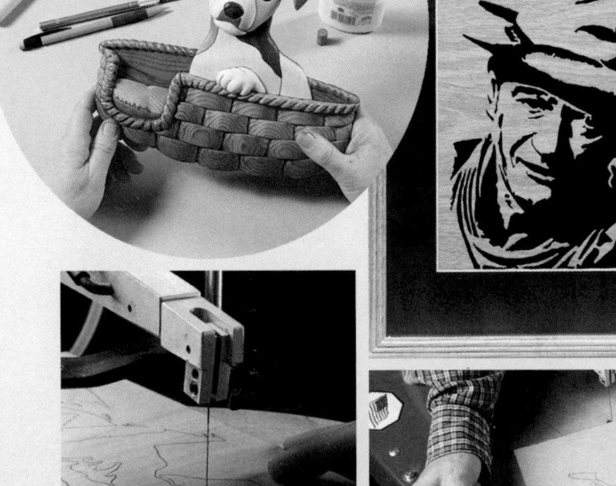

Each full color issue will contain:

- **Ready to use patterns**
- **Straight talk tool reviews**
- **Step by step instructions**
- **Poor Man's money-saving tips**
- **Hands-on info for every scroller, from beginner to advanced**

Future Issues will feature:

- *Pattern projects by Patrick Spielman*
- *Holiday ornament patterns*
- *The secrets of Corian® scrolling*
- *Getting the most from your scroll saw blades*
- *The Columbine Crosses: A story of healing*
- *Scroll Saw School Report*

SCROLL SAW TOYS AND VEHICLES

SCROLL SAW TOYS & VEHICLES
By Stan Graves

FREE with a 2-year paid subscription!
42 Pages, 8.5 x 11 soft cover

Includes:
- *Sturdy, practical designs*
- *Ready-to-use patterns for 10 vehicles*
- *Full-color photographs of the finished projects*

✔ YES, START MY SUBSCRIPTION RIGHT AWAY!

CALL TOLL-FREE 1-800-457-9112

BEST VALUE

2 YEARS (8 ISSUES)
- ☐ **$39.90 U.S.**
- ☐ $45.00 Canada (US Funds only)
- ☐ $55.90 International (US Funds only)

1 YEAR (4 ISSUES)
- ☐ **$19.95 U.S.**
- ☐ $22.50 Canada (US Funds only)
- ☐ $27.95 International (US Funds only)

Please allow 4-6 weeks for delivery of your first issue.

NAME ____
ADDRESS ____
CITY ____ STATE/PROV ____ ZIP/PC ____
PHONE ____
E-MAIL ____

VISA MasterCard DISCOVER NOVUS

Name on Card ____ Exp. Date ____

Card Number ____

Send your order form with check or money order to: SSW Subscriptions • 1970 Broad Street • East Petersburg, PA 17520

Or order online at: www.scrollsawer.com

158-9